THE ROAD OF A DREAMER

The Road of a Dreamer

HECTOR A IBARRA

THE ROAD
OF A
DREAMER

DISCLAIMER

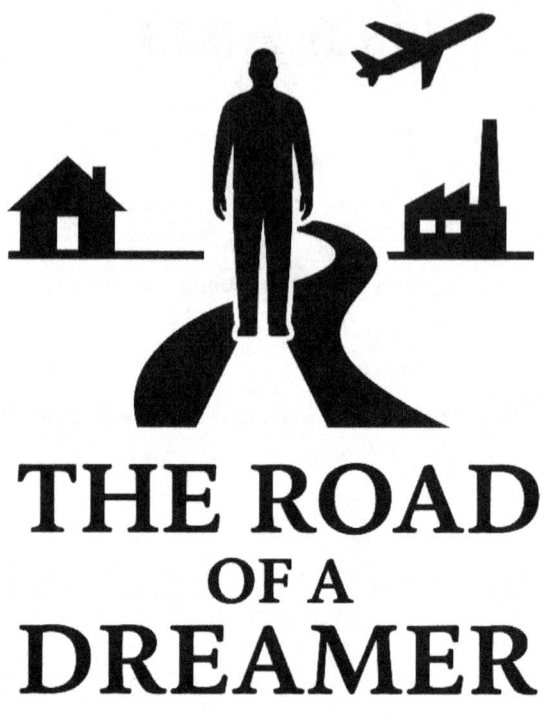

THE ROAD
OF A
DREAMER

Some roads are paved with certainty. Others, like mine, are carved step by step through perseverance, faith, and a dream that refused to die. From a dusty childhood in Piedras Negras to a quiet goodbye at the U.S. border, I've learned that resilience is not built overnight—it's shaped by family, failure, and the hope for something better.

The Road of a Dreamer is not a story of perfection. It's a story of falling forward—of being a boy who talked too much, a teen who loved too hard, a man who carried his father's lessons, and a leader who walked into fire so others wouldn't have to.

In these pages, I share not just what I lived, but what I felt. And I hope that wherever you are on your own road, you'll find a little light in mine.

TABLE OF CONTENTS

DEDICATION

To my wife, Patty, whose unwavering love and belief in me has been an anchor through every chapter of life.

To my daughter Anna, whose curiosity, compassion, and strength continue to inspire me.

To the memory of my father, whose quiet resilience and hard work laid the foundation of my dreams.

To my mother and brothers, whose support and shared history gave me the courage to forge my own path.

And to every friend, mentor, and coworker who crossed my journey – thank you for leaving your mark on my story.

This book is not only about one dreamer's road – it's about all of those who walked besides him.

CHAPTER 1: EARLY CHILDHOOD IN PIEDRAS NEGRAS

I was born in Piedras Negras, Coahuila, a small border town on the edge of Mexico and the United States. My earliest memories are wrapped in the dusty warmth of our neighborhood, where kids played barefoot in the streets until the sun dipped below the horizon.

Life was simple, rooted in strong family values and unspoken rules of respect and resilience. My parents were firm yet loving, and the bond between me and my brothers was forged through countless adventures and shared mischief.

Family was always a central pillar in my life. Growing up in Piedras Negras, I was the eldest of three brothers. My parents were loving but hardworking, each playing a unique and vital role in shaping who I would become.

Before my father became known for his years at the Wrangler jeans factory, he had an entirely different path. He studied and worked as a survey engineer—a profession that shaped his discipline, technical mind, and meticulous attention to detail.

In those early days, my dad would often be seen in the open fields of Coahuila, armed with a theodolite, measuring land boundaries with precision. He had a love for geometry and calculations, but more than that, he admired structure and planning. The way he approached surveying was not just about numbers; it was about helping shape the future of developing communities.

His job as a surveyor was demanding. He would often leave before dawn and return well into the evening, sunburned and tired, but with a quiet sense of accomplishment. He would bring home stories about working in remote areas, dealing with difficult terrain, and the camaraderie built among his team. This experience instilled in him a sense of resilience and work ethic that he would carry with him throughout his life.

When the opportunity came to work at the Wrangler jeans factory, it wasn't initially what he had in mind. It was a pivot, but one he made not out of disappointment but out of necessity and love for his family. The steady job at Wrangler offered stability, and he welcomed the change. What's remarkable is how he applied the same engineering mindset to his work on the factory floor. He learned every process, understood the machinery, and always looked for ways to make operations smoother and more efficient.

At Wrangler, he wasn't just a worker—he became a reliable part of the company. His background in surveying gave him a unique edge; he understood systems, patterns, and the importance of precision. Whether it was aligning the stitching on a pair of jeans or planning a shift schedule, he did it with purpose.

Looking back, I believe that being a survey engineer was more than a job—it laid the foundation for who he was. It taught him how to observe, plan, and persevere. Those qualities stayed with him through his entire career, from open land to factory floors. He always said life is about adapting, and he lived that truth. From calculating land elevations to helping make the jeans worn by everyday people, he shaped both landscapes and lives.

Back then, Wrangler jeans were not just a fashion statement—they were a symbol of durability, of hard work, and of pride. My father was one of the many skilled workers who spent long hours making sure every stitch, every seam, and every rivet was done to perfection. He didn't design them, and he didn't sell them, but he helped bring them to life.

He worked with the machines that cut and sewed the denim, often surrounded by the constant hum of industrial sewing machines and the sharp, familiar scent of denim and machine oil. It was repetitive work, physically demanding and mentally numbing at times, but he never complained. He had a quiet dignity about his job—he was contributing to something tangible, something people wore every day.

The Wrangler factory was also where my father first developed his eye for quality. He would later take this skill with him to General Motors, where he transitioned from sewing machines to automotive assembly lines and eventually became a Quality Manager. But the foundation was built in that jeans factory.

He once told me that working at Wrangler taught him the value of doing the little things right—the tiny adjustments, the unseen efforts that make a big difference in the final product. That lesson stuck with me. Whether I was quoting a project as an engineer or managing a full production plant, I always thought about the "invisible" work that leads to visible results.

Looking back, I see that part of my work ethic and respect for the manufacturing process was rooted in watching my father come home from the Wrangler factory. It was more than just denim. It was discipline. It was craftsmanship. It was pride in a job well done.

My brothers Alex and Jorge were closer in age, which naturally brought them closer together. I often found myself on the outside of their camaraderie, which pushed me to engage with older people. It wasn't long before I discovered I was more comfortable talking with adults than with kids my age. I wasn't shy—in fact, I was outgoing and curious. I loved conversation, storytelling, and learning from the experiences of others.

One particular memory stands out from when I was very young. My room had a window that faced the street. One night, my mother noticed a woman staring through it. Alarmed, she called my father. The woman was taken to a mental health facility, and it was later discovered that she had been watching me for several nights. I don't remember it myself, but the vivid way my mother told the story made it feel like a part of my own memory.

Despite this unsettling moment, most of my early memories are joyful and full of curiosity. I remember participating in a singing contest at a local radio station. My mother had heard about it and encouraged me to try. I sang "El Rey" by José Alfredo Jiménez, standing confidently in front of a live audience with music playing behind me. When I came home with my prize—three long-play records from Cepillín, a beloved children's entertainer—I felt like a champion. That moment solidified something in me: I was never afraid of an audience, a stage, or a microphone.

These early experiences made it clear that I had a gift for communication. I could express myself, hold attention, and connect with people. I didn't worry about being laughed at or judged. I just enjoyed the interaction. Communication wasn't just talking—it was sharing ideas, connecting emotionally, and letting people see who I was.

As I look back, these formative years laid the foundation for many things: my eventual love of public speaking, my confidence in leadership roles, and my natural inclination toward storytelling. They were the seeds of a life-long journey to connect, inspire, and reflect.

Piedras Negras was also the backdrop for my early experiments in mischief. When I was around 7 or 8 years old, my friends and I armed ourselves with BB guns and set out to "hunt" the glass Coca-Cola bottles stacked behind the factory. We'd hide and shoot until someone would yell, "Get those kids!" and we'd run like hell, laughing all the way home. We were lucky we never got caught. That same year, one of our friends brought a single beer to a treehouse, and we decided to share it using straws. The result? Drunken dizziness. I couldn't even climb down. We had to wait until the world stopped spinning. That was one of only a few times I've ever been drunk in my life.

One day, my uncle noticed something blinking in the sky. Curious, we grabbed one of my dad's surveying tools—a theodolite—and took turns looking through it. What we saw was like something out of science fiction: a silver, diamond-shaped object with lights at its center. Soon, neighbors gathered on our porch to see it. The local newspaper even reported on it, calling it a UFO sighting by Mr. Ibarra. Crossing the border to Eagle Pass afterward, U.S. agents would sometimes ask sarcastically, "You the UFO guy?" My dad would just laugh and say, "Well, that's what the paper said." Years later, when I watched *Close Encounters of the Third Kind,* it all came flooding back. I still don't know what we saw that day, but it was one of those stories that are embedded in my memory from living in Piedras Negras.

These moments shaped my early years—moments of joy, fear, curiosity, and a constant sense of wonder. They were the first bricks in the foundation of the person I would become.

CHAPTER 2: YOU WANTED THE BEST, YOU GOT THE BEST

I was seven years old and living in Piedras Negras when I first encountered something that would change the way I saw the world—KISS. It was a quiet evening in our modest living room. The television, a bulky box with rabbit-ear antennas wrapped in foil, glowed with colors that always seemed a little off. My brothers and I were huddled close, flipping through the limited channels we had access to, when suddenly—there they were.

Four men, dressed in leather and spikes, faces painted like living comic book heroes, playing rock music with fire and fury I had never imagined possible. I was frozen. Their name appeared in bold, electrified letters—KISS. They were theatrical, loud, rebellious, and completely captivating. I didn't understand a word of what they were singing, but it didn't matter. Something inside me lit up. I had to know more. I had to own that feeling.

A few days later, still buzzing with excitement, I asked my mom if I could buy a record from Kiss. She learned from a friend in the neighborhood that there was a teenager a few blocks away who not only had KISS albums but also a collection of posters and pictures. With my small savings—mostly coins I had stashed away in a little box—we went to see him. His room was like a shrine to the band. Posters of Gene Simmons breathing fire, Paul Stanley with his starry eye makeup, Ace Frehley looking like a space alien, and Peter Criss behind his drum kit surrounded the walls.

I told him I wanted to buy something—anything—to feel connected to what I had seen. He looked through his stack and pulled out a copy of "Dynasty." The cover art alone was hypnotizing. He told me it was one of their latest albums and showed me some pictures that came with it. With all the seriousness of a seven-year-old on a sacred mission, I handed over my savings. The record was mine.

I ran home clutching it like treasure. Just holding the vinyl and studying every detail of the cover gave me immense joy. Eventually, I managed to play it, and as the music spun, it felt like my world had gotten just a little bit bigger. That moment, in Piedras Negras, was the beginning of my lifelong love of music and storytelling.

KISS wasn't just a band—they were larger than life. And to a little boy growing up on the border, they were a portal into a world where expression had no limits.

CHAPTER 3: ONE OF THE BIG THREE MOVES TO SALTILLO

Leaving Piedras Negras was one of the first major transitions of my life. I was still a child when my family decided it was time to move to Saltillo. At that age, change can feel like an adventure, but it can also be unsettling. Piedras Negras had been my home, my playground, and the setting for my earliest memories—from riding my bike down dusty streets to playing with my cousins and attending elementary school with familiar faces. It was a place where everything and everyone felt known and safe.

The decision to move came from my parents' desire to provide a better life and more opportunities for their children. My father, a hardworking man, had ambitions that reached beyond the borders of our small town. He saw Saltillo not only as a bigger city with more economic potential but also as a place where his children could access better education and a more structured path toward a professional future.

I remember one road trip that stood out during my childhood. We were traveling from Piedras Negras to Saltillo, and our bus had to pass through a treacherous mountain area called La Muralla, between Monclova and Saltillo. Known for deadly accidents and winding roads, it terrified me. The bus driver, perhaps trying to impress or scare us, pointed to a ravine and said, "You see down there? A bus fell. Everyone died." Whether it was true or not, the fear stuck with me. We traveled that road often, and each time my heart would pound.

I remember the day we finally packed our belongings. My brothers and I were both excited and nervous. The idea of moving to a new city sounded like an adventure at first—new streets to explore, new schools, new friends. But there was also fear. What if the kids at the new school didn't like me? What if I couldn't fit in?

The drive to Saltillo was long and quiet. My father kept his focus on the road, my mother looking out the window with a mixture of sadness and anticipation in her eyes. I sat in the back seat wondering what our new home would look like, trying to picture a future that was still blurry in my imagination.

When we arrived in Saltillo, it was nothing like Piedras Negras. The air felt different—cooler, less dusty. The city was larger, more modern, and far more intimidating to a young boy used to the small-town rhythm of life. The houses were built closer together, the schools were bigger, and the streets were louder. I felt small again, like I had been dropped into a new world where the rules hadn't been explained.

The first days at my new school were tough. I was shy and uncertain, missing my old friends and teachers. But little by little, I began to adapt. I discovered that Saltillo had its own kind of charm—rich culture, historical buildings, and kind-hearted people who, once they got to know you, treated you like family.

Our new house in Saltillo became the place where many of the formative experiences of my youth would unfold. It was in Saltillo where I fell in love for the first time, got into trouble at my Catholic high school, began to dream of becoming a sound engineer, and eventually decided on the path of Industrial Engineering. It was a place of transformation—not just for me, but for our entire family.

Looking back, that move was the first of many bold steps that shaped my journey. It was a reminder that sometimes, the discomfort of change is the birthplace of growth. And even though I left a piece of my childhood behind in Piedras Negras, I carried with me the roots that would keep me grounded in every new place I'd call home.

The move had been a significant change, but Saltillo was a growing city filled with new opportunities. One of the most impactful developments during this time was the establishment of the General Motors factory in Saltillo. It would change not only the economic landscape of the region, but also the direction of our family's life.

General Motors was looking for talented and experienced professionals to help build and manage their state-of-the-art manufacturing plant. It was a bold and strategic move that aligned with the growing wave of industrial development in northern Mexico. The automotive industry was expanding, and Saltillo's location made it an ideal hub for production and distribution throughout the continent.

When my father was hired as a Quality Manager, it was a moment of great pride for our entire family. He had worked tirelessly throughout his life, and now he was being recognized by one of the largest companies in the world. His role was pivotal. He wasn't just overseeing quality; he was helping to establish the very foundations of how quality would be defined and measured in this new plant.

As children, we didn't fully grasp the scale of what he was doing, but we could feel the difference. He carried a sense of responsibility that was both inspiring and humbling. He was part of something much bigger now—something that would define an era in Saltillo's industrial journey.

My father's new position brought stability to our home, but it also came with sacrifice. He would often come home late, tired but satisfied, talking about inspections, specifications, and the importance of doing things right the first time. He taught us that quality wasn't just about work—it was a value, a way of life.

Over time, General Motors became one of the region's most important employers, and my father's contributions were a piece of that legacy. His discipline, passion for learning, and work ethic helped shape not just the standards of the plant, but the future opportunities for many families in Saltillo.

Looking back, I now realize how much of my own career path was influenced by watching him in those years. He wasn't just building cars—he was building a better life for us and showing me the road, I would one day walk myself.

CHAPTER 4: CAPTAIN CAVEMAN

"It's not what they call you, it's what you answer to." – My mother's sage advice, offered when I was twelve, echoed in my mind for years. At the time, I wasn't so sure I believed it. In middle school, names have a way of sticking to you like glue, whether you answer to them or not.

I first earned the nickname "Captain Caveman" on an otherwise unremarkable autumn afternoon in sixth grade. The bell had just rung for lunch, and I was hurrying out to the soccer field. My friend Vladimir came bounding up behind me and, out of nowhere, gave a loud, comical shout: "Captain CAAAAAAVEMAAAAN!" His voice echoed off the metal lockers. I froze in place as a few heads turned our way. My cheeks burned with confusion and mild embarrassment. Vladimir was grinning from ear to ear, clearly amused with himself. I had no idea what he was talking about.

As we went to the patio, I asked him, "Why did you yell 'Captain Caveman'? Who is that supposed to be?" Vladimir could barely contain his laughter. "Dude, have you never seen the old cartoon?" he chortled. Seeing my blank expression, he launched into an explanation: Captain Caveman was a goofy prehistoric superhero from some vintage Hanna-Barbera show, a short, hairy caveman with a club who yelled his own name as a battle cry. Earlier that day I had been hunched over my desk, my long shaggy hair nearly covering my eyes as I furiously scribbled notes. Vladimir thought I looked exactly like the cartoon caveman about to attack his notebook. Thus, on a whim, the nickname was born.

I gave a faint, ha-ha very funny kind of chuckle and tried to act unbothered. But inside, I felt a twinge of self-consciousness. At twelve, the last thing you want is to be compared to a prehistoric cartoon character. I remember running my fingers through my thick brown hair, realizing it had grown pretty unruly. That night, I stood an extra few minutes in front of the mirror. Was my jaw really that square? Were my eyebrows that bushy? In truth I was an early bloomer – already a bit taller and, yes, hairier than some of my classmates. My mom said I was just "maturing quickly," but in middle school that just meant fresh ammunition for teasing.

Over the next few days, Vladimir's little joke caught on faster than I could have imagined. In the hallways, I'd hear the occasional grunt or someone humming the Flintstones theme when I walked by. A couple of jokesters from my homeroom started greeting me by pounding their chests and saying "Ugh! Ugh!" like cavemen. It was mortifying and a bit funny all at once. I tried to laugh along, but each time I heard "Caveman!" echo behind me, I felt a swirl of emotions — equal parts amusement, embarrassment, and annoyance.

What made it worse was that even people who weren't my friends started using the nickname. It had escaped into the wider school ecosystem. In gym class, when sides were picked for soccer, someone yelled, "I want Caveman on my team!" and a ripple of laughter went through the group. I half-expected the coach to start using it. Thankfully, most teachers stuck to my real name, but the damage was done: everyone in the seventh grade knew who Captain Caveman was, and that it was me.

At home, I pretended everything was normal. I didn't tell my parents about the nickname right away. Part of me feared they'd overreact and call the school, which would only make things worse. Another part of me was oddly ashamed — as if I had done something to invite this label. When my mom eventually heard the name (overhearing Vladimir calling me "Caveman" when he came home to visit), she sat me down to ask about it. "They call you Captain Caveman? Why?" she asked gently, clearly concerned it was mean-spirited. I shrugged, playing it cool. "It's just a stupid joke, Ma. Because of my hair, I guess." I forced a laugh. "It's no big deal."

That's when she gave me the advice I'd carry for years: "Remember, it doesn't matter what they call you. It matters what you answer to." She ruffled my shaggy hair and added with a wink, "But maybe a haircut wouldn't hurt." I managed a real laugh at that. That night, I seriously considered taking her up on the haircut suggestion — as if taming my hair could erase the Caveman moniker. In the end I only trimmed it a bit. Deep down, I knew a simple haircut wouldn't rewrite my peers' perception of me overnight. The name had stuck like gum to a shoe.

Despite my outward nonchalance, Captain Caveman weighed on me. I worried: Is this all people see when they look at me? A cartoonish caveman caricature? In class, I found myself participating less, afraid that if I said something wrong someone would grunt or tease, "Caveman smash!" When you're a kid, a nickname can feel like a costume you didn't choose to wear — and I wasn't sure if I could ever take it off.

My first year in a Saltillo school was sixth grade on elementary. This was the last year before we were moving to middle school.

It was the sixth-grade graduation trip—the one we'd all been buzzing about for weeks. We were finally going to leave behind our uniforms, classrooms, and strict teachers for a few days of freedom and fun. Our destination was several places in central Mexico, and although it was just a several hours away, for a bunch of twelve-year-olds, it felt like crossing into another country.

The moment we arrived, the chaos began. There was something electric in the air—freedom, excitement, the first real taste of independence. We were separated into groups and assigned hotel rooms. The guys all dropped their bags and immediately started claiming beds, shouting over each other, laughing, and running around like wild animals.

And then there was Lucas.

Lucas was one of those kids who made himself a perfect target without even trying. He was quiet, a little too shy. Naturally, that made him the victim of many jokes. But the one that would go down in school legend was the prank we pulled on him that first night.

He had left his change of clothes on his bed and gone to the showers. That's when the idea struck—simple, mischievous, and perfect. We grabbed his clothes and tossed them directly into the giant industrial fan that was in our room's ceiling. The moment the blades whirred to life, his shirt took off like a ghost in flight. His socks got caught and flapped like little flags. His underwear? Well, let's just say it achieved lift-off. Everyone was howling with laughter.

When Lucas came back, towel around his waist, looking for his clothes, we pretended not to know a thing. But the smirks and stifled laughter gave us away. The look on his face when he realized what had happened—part fury, part disbelief—was priceless. He stormed off trying to collect what he could find, and although he was mad, even he cracked a smile later that night.

That same night, something else unforgettable happened—my first kiss.

After dinner, our teachers let us go to a movie in the hotel theater. As the lights dimmed, everyone started to shift around, trying to sit closer to their crushes, pretending it was for a better view of the screen.

Paola was sitting next to me. She was quiet, kind, and had the most mesmerizing eyes I'd ever seen. I had a crush on her for months but never dared to say a word. Somehow, that night, with the buzz of the day still in the air and the freedom of being away from home, I found myself sliding over to where she sat.

We didn't talk much. Just a few shy words, nervous laughter, and then, during a slow, emotional part of the movie, she looked at me and smiled. I felt my heart pound. And then, quietly, as if it had been scripted in some coming-of-age film, she leaned closer. So did I. And there it was—my first kiss. Sweet, innocent, clumsy, and unforgettable.

When the movie ended, we both pretended like nothing had happened. But I couldn't stop smiling. It felt like something had shifted. That day had started with a prank and ended with something that felt like magic. In many ways, that trip marked the beginning of growing up—of realizing how complex, hilarious, and heartwarming life could be, all in a single day.

Captain Caveman was on a roll.

By the time I graduated middle school, I was determined to leave Captain Caveman behind me. I looked forward to high school as a fresh start — a chance to be seen as me, not as a walking punchline. That summer before ninth grade, I even begged my parents to let me switch to a different high school than most of my middle school peers. No luck. The district lines were set, and so was my fate: many of the same kids would be joining me in ninth grade come September.

On the first day of high school, I walked through the towering front gates of Colegio Mexico with equal parts excitement and dread. I had a new backpack, new sneakers, and a freshly ironed shirt. I'd also finally gotten a shorter haircut — a very deliberate, neat style that I hoped would distance me from any caveman comparisons. For a few moments, as I navigated the morning crowds, I felt like any other nervous freshman. No one was pointing or laughing. I was just me, an anonymous 14-year-old among hundreds of others. It was liberating.

That illusion shattered by lunchtime. I was standing in the cafeteria queue when I heard it: "Yo, Captain Caveman! Over here!" The voice rang out above the dull roar of student chatter. My stomach dropped. I turned slowly to see who it was. At a table near the window, Vladimir and a couple of other guys from my old school were waving me over. One of them was pounding an invisible club in his hand with a goofy grin. A few unfamiliar students glanced toward me, curious about the nickname. My face flushed hot. I remember closing my eyes for a split second, as if I could will myself invisible or rewind time and respond to Vladimir's shout with a different reaction.

I had a choice: I could ignore them — pretend I didn't hear — or I could walk over, face it head on. A few kids snickered, and I even heard someone whisper, "Is that caveman guy for real?" Resilience wasn't a word in my vocabulary then, but something in me decided not to run away. With a deep breath and a forced smirk, I grabbed my lunch tray and marched over to Vladimir's table. "What's up, guys," I muttered, sliding into a seat. I tried to sound casual, but I couldn't quite meet their eyes at first. Vladimir clapped me on the back, oblivious to my discomfort. "Dude, we were just talking about the new history teacher. Thought of you when he mentioned the Stone Age," he joked. More laughter. I poked at my sandwich, mustering a halfhearted chuckle.

Over the next few weeks, Captain Caveman resurfaced as if it had been lurking just around the corner, waiting for the right moment to pounce. Some older students got wind of it and, to my surprise, a couple actually found it entertaining in a friendly way. One of the senior guys on the soccer team heard someone call me Caveman in the hallway. Instead of mocking me, he seemed impressed. "Caveman? That's badass," he said, giving me a fist bump. "You play any sports? We could use a caveman on the defensive line." I was taken aback — I'd never played football or rugby, and I was more of a bookish type — but his reaction weirdly made me feel a little proud rather than ashamed. It was the first time I realized a nickname, even a silly one, could be interpreted differently depending on who's using it.

Still, there were plenty of times in early high school when the nickname hurt. Sophomore year, I overheard a girl I had a crush on ask her friend, "Why do they call him caveman? Is it because he's kinda... rough-looking?" I wanted to sink into the floor. That comment gnawed at my self-esteem. I started worrying more about my appearance. I kept my hair trimmed short, and updated my wardrobe to something trendier than the baggy jeans and oversized t-shirts I wore in middle school. I figured if I looked less like the stereotype, the name might fade.

It didn't fade. If anything, it evolved. Some friends just shortened it to "Caver." By junior year, a lot of people actually thought my last name was Caver — I remember one of my schoolmates was shocked to learn it wasn't. "Wait, that's just a nickname? I thought it was, like, your real name or something!" she exclaimed. We both ended up laughing. By then, Captain Caveman had become such an established part of my high school identity that even I would sometimes shake my head and smile at the absurdity of it.

Heading off to college was another chance to reinvent myself, and this time I had a choice: I could finally bury Captain Caveman for good, or carry him with me as a funny part of my past. When I arrived at UANE, nobody knew about my alter ego. In the first few weeks of freshman year, I introduced myself by my given name, joined study groups, made friends in the dorms, and enjoyed the freedom of being just an ordinary guy again. It felt liberating that for the first time in years, I wasn't "the caveman" to anyone.

Oddly enough, I found that I missed parts of it. Not the teasing or the embarrassment, of course. What I missed was the easy ice-breaker it had been or the camaraderie it sometimes brought. In high school, anyone could joke with me by invoking Caveman, and it created an instant bond or laugh. Now, in college, I actually chose to share the story behind my nickname with new friends. Usually it came up in late-night dorm conversations, the kind where everyone swaps high school war stories. "You think you had it bad," I'd say with a grin, "try walking around with 'Captain Caveman' as your nickname for six years." This would be met with incredulous laughter, and inevitably someone would start calling me Caveman in jest. But here's the difference: I was in control of the narrative now. I was sharing it on my own terms, almost like a goofy badge of honor.

College wasn't all silliness and parties, though. In quieter moments, as I studied in the library or walked the campus alone, I'd reflect on the journey from that self-conscious seventh grader to the person I was now. I realized that the nickname itself wasn't what shaped me – it was how I reacted to it, how I let it affect me, and eventually how I chose to rise above it (and even embrace it) that shaped me. In psychology class, we learned about the concept of labels and self-identity. I wrote a term paper on how nicknames and labels in adolescence can influence self-esteem and behavior. It was more than just academic for me; it was deeply personal. I argued that while a nickname can initially mold how you see yourself (I certainly had moments when I wondered if "caveman" was all I'd ever be seen as), ultimately we have the power to redefine those labels — or peel them off entirely and show what's underneath.

Looking back now, I see Captain Caveman as a defining chapter of my life for all the right reasons. It taught me about who I was and who

I refused to be. In middle school, I let a label define me; I shrunk under its weight, allowing it to chip away at my confidence. In high school, I learned to own it, to wear it lightly like a costume I could take on and off. And in college, I finally understood that I was never obligated to wear it at all — I chose to, when it suited me, because it had become a quirky, lovable part of my story.

That nickname journey also taught me a great deal about resilience. Kids slung a label at me, and it stuck. But instead of letting it wound me forever, I gradually developed a thicker skin and a stronger sense of self. I had to, if I wanted to survive adolescence with my sanity intact. There's a saying that floated around in my head during those years (maybe from a poster in the school counselor's office, or something my mom said): "Sticks and stones may break my bones, but words will never hurt me." I remember scoffing at that line whenever I heard it – because the truth is, words can hurt, especially when you're young and trying to figure out your identity. Each "Caveman" taunt in seventh grade did sting, at least a little. But with time I learned that while words can hurt, they don't have to define you.

I also learned about the kindness of true friends through this experience. Vladimir, who first gave me the nickname, turned out not to be a villain in my life story, but a friend who simply didn't realize the impact of his joke. When I finally told him, sometime around tenth grade, that I sometimes hated being called Captain Caveman, he was genuinely surprised. "I always thought you were okay with it, you know? You always laughed it off," he said, apologetic. That opened up one of the most honest conversations we ever had. He even started using my real name more often after that, at least when he sensed I'd had enough Caveman for one day. It wasn't a perfect fix, but it meant a lot. It showed me that sometimes people don't know the weight of the words they throw at you — and that a little communication can lighten the load.

As I write this chapter of my life, I do so with a smile. Who would have thought that a silly cartoon caveman would play such a pivotal role in my journey of self-discovery? Life has a funny way of using the most unexpected things to teach us resilience and confidence. In my case, it used a nickname – one that at first I wanted to escape, but eventually came to terms with. Captain Caveman will always be a part of my story, but it's not the whole story.

In the end, I came to understand the truth of my mother's advice years ago. It took growing up and gaining confidence in myself to really get it. It isn't what they call you that truly matters — it's what you answer to. I was called Captain Caveman, and I answered to it for a while, even let it define me for a time. But ultimately, I answered to a higher call — the call to define myself on my own terms. That is the identity I embrace and carry forward. And that, more than any nickname or label, is the truest reflection of who I am.

CHAPTER 5: FIRST LOVE, ANOTHER BRICK IN COLMEX

High school years were filled with new experiences and important lessons that would shape my understanding of relationships and emotions. It was during this time, at Colegio Mexico, a Catholic school, that I first truly fell in love.

Her name isn't important now, but I remember everything about her. She was blonde, had large expressive eyes, and a warm smile that made her stand out even though, objectively, she wasn't the prettiest girl in school. There was something about her that captivated me from the moment she walked into our classroom. She was new to our school, having just arrived from the Dominican Republic. Her quiet demeanor and radiant presence made her unforgettable.

I wasted no time. I was never shy and wasn't about to start now. I sat next to her and began building a connection. After several days of talking and sharing stories, I asked her to be my girlfriend—and to my great surprise, she said yes. That moment became the spark of what I believed at the time was a love that could last forever.

We were inseparable. We spent countless hours talking on the phone, going out to restaurants with the help of our parents who would drive us, and exchanging letters and small gifts. I was committed to her with all the heart and intensity of a sixteen-year-old. We never crossed the line into anything intimate, but emotionally we were deeply involved. We shared secrets, hopes, and dreams. She became a constant part of my world.

However, I was young, immature, and possessive. I wanted her all to myself. When she began making more friends and wanting to expand her social circle, I didn't handle it well. Jealousy overtook reason. I became controlling without realizing how much I was pushing her away. Eventually, the pressure was too much for her, and she ended our relationship. I was devastated. Angry. Hurt. And worst of all, I knew the reason it ended was because of me.

What made things worse was having to see her every day at school. I had introduced her to my circle of friends, and now I felt betrayed seeing her laugh and talk with them like nothing had changed. In a moment of immaturity, I asked my friends to choose between her and me—an unfair and selfish ultimatum. They refused to take sides, telling me that it wasn't right to force them into a decision like that. I didn't take it well. Instead of accepting the situation, I made the choice for them and distanced myself from all of them.

It was one of the loneliest periods of my life. I lost a girlfriend and a group of friends all at once. But through that pain, I learned some of the most important lessons about relationships and about myself.

First, I learned that we don't own anyone. Love cannot be possessive. People stay in our lives because they choose to—not because we demand it. Relationships must be built on trust and respect, not control.

Second, I learned that dragging others into personal conflicts only spreads the damage. Asking people to choose sides in emotional battles only ends up hurting more people and often leaves you more isolated than before.

And finally, I learned that sometimes, the best thing you can do is simply walk away. Trying to force something that's broken only deepens the wounds.

That relationship didn't last, but the lessons it gave me have remained. They became part of the foundation I would use later to build healthier, more respectful relationships. Sometimes heartbreak is a painful teacher—but one that leaves behind wisdom worth carrying for a lifetime.

But I don't only remember Colegio Mexico for my first love and heartbreak; oh no, there was a lot more than that.

When I first set foot in Colegio México, I was a mix of curiosity and nerves, dressed in the classic uniform of navy pants, white shirt, and a tie that felt more like a noose than part of school pride. The school was strict, rooted in Catholic tradition, and run by priests who expected discipline, reverence, and silence. I could manage the first two, but silence? That was always my downfall.

From a young age, I was talkative — some might say too talkative. I saw conversation as a sport, a way to connect, make people laugh, and sometimes (much to the annoyance of my teachers) a way to kill time during boring classes. At Colegio México, though, this trait was quickly flagged as a problem. The priests believed that silence was the path to virtue. I, however, believed that laughter was.

My troubles began innocently enough — whispering to a friend during mass, cracking a joke during morning announcements, mimicking a teacher's voice under my breath. But it escalated. Soon, I was earning myself regular visits to the head priest's office. It didn't matter that my grades were decent or that I never skipped class. In their eyes, I was the class clown. And for that, I had to pay the price.

Discipline at Colegio México came in many forms. There was the usual: staying after school to clean the classroom, writing lines ("I will not speak without permission" a hundred times), or losing your recess time to stand outside the teacher's lounge with your hands behind your back.

The priests had their own unique ways of dealing with students like me. A regular punishment was being sent out to the patio to do laps. I remember many afternoons spent running in circles under the hot sun, sometimes even with a stack of books in my arms. One particularly memorable time, I was assigned to do laps with Paola (yes, my first kiss, after that night, we had become great friends) — a punishment that didn't feel like a punishment at all. We ended up chatting and laughing more than sweating, and though it started as discipline, it ended in one of my fondest memories.

Despite the trouble I got into, Colegio México taught me important lessons. Discipline, for one. I learned that being clever wasn't enough — timing mattered, as did self-control. I also learned how to charm my way out of deeper trouble. I became a master of sincere-sounding apologies and innocent expressions.

There were moments when the punishments felt excessive, but even then, I never felt unloved. The priests, strict as they were, never gave up on me. They believed that inside the class clown was a student with potential — a mischievous spirit that just needed direction.

Looking back, I treasure those days. Colegio México shaped me in ways I didn't understand at the time. It was the place where I first learned to question authority (and sometimes pay for it), where I learned the power of words — to provoke, to unite, and to entertain. It was where I realized that even within rules, there's room for personality, for laughter, and for rebellion — so long as you're willing to face the consequences.

And it was where I began to understand something bigger: that every label has layers. I wasn't just the talker, the troublemaker, or the joker. I was a young man in formation — learning who I was through the boundaries I pushed and the rules I broke.

In that sacred, chalk-dusted school, surrounded by saints' statues and stern priests, I found my first real audience. And though I often stood in front of them for the wrong reasons, those moments helped me find my voice — a voice I'd later use not to disrupt, but to lead.

It was a warm afternoon at Colegio México, and I was sitting in one of the old wooden desks in our psychology class, taught by a priest whose name I've long forgotten, but whose lesson has stayed with me for life. This was no ordinary theology lecture, no rote memorization of virtues or saints. On that particular day, the priest walked into the room wheeling a TV cart with a VHS player and a few dusty speakers — a rare sight that meant only one thing: we were going to watch a movie. The title? The Wall by Pink Floyd.

At first, I thought it was some kind of mistake. Why would a Catholic priest, in our conservative school, show us a film filled with angst, symbolism, and rebellion? But he assured us: "Today, we're going to take a journey — not to the outside world, but into yourselves."

I had always loved music, but The Wall wasn't just music. It was an experience — abstract, intense, confusing, but deeply emotional. We sat there watching the surreal visuals: the marching hammers, the faceless schoolmasters, the screaming heads, the sense of isolation and emotional walls built brick by brick. As a teenager trying to figure out the world and my place in it, it hit me in ways I didn't fully understand at the time.

When the movie ended, there was silence. The priest turned off the TV, then looked around and said something I'll never forget: "Each one of you is building a wall. Around your fears, your traumas, your disappointments. Some of you use anger, others use sarcasm or silence. But you're all doing it."

He then asked us to write down — not for him, but for ourselves — what bricks we were stacking in our own walls. It was the first time anyone had asked me to reflect like that, not as a student, but as a person.

I don't remember what I wrote, but I do remember how I felt. Vulnerable. Seen. Confused. Honest.

That class taught me something deeper than any textbook. It showed me that even the hardest people often carry soft wounds, and that rebellion isn't always about noise — sometimes it's a quiet cry for understanding. In a school where rules were strict and discipline was expected, that priest gave us space for introspection — and used rock music, no less, to do it.

Years later, whenever I hear Comfortably Numb or Another Brick in the Wall, I'm transported back to that classroom. I can still hear the echoes of the priest's voice, asking us to look inside ourselves, not just at the grades on our report cards.

Of all the lessons I learned in high school, that one might've been the most important — and the one I carry with me still.

CHAPTER 6: A NEW PATH AND THE POWER OF PASSION

As high school progressed, I found myself at a crossroads where I had to decide what I wanted to do with my life. I had a strong passion for music and dreamed of becoming a sound engineer—someone who works the console at concerts or in studios, ensuring that every sound is just right. The idea of creating sonic experiences for others, being behind the scenes of the music I loved, was thrilling.

Excited about the possibility, I approached my father with the idea. He listened carefully, as he always did, and then responded with his usual measured wisdom. "If you were living in the United States," he said, "that could be a good career. But here in Mexico, you'll struggle to find a job doing that. You need to think about something more practical, something that will give you stability."

Disappointed but understanding his concern, I started to think about other paths. My dad suggested I consider Industrial Engineering—a field he was familiar with through his own career at General Motors. He said it was versatile and in demand. The idea of improving systems, solving problems, and working with people intrigued me. So, I chose to pursue Industrial Engineering. My dream of being involved in music didn't disappear—it simply became something I would explore as a hobby. I took his advice seriously and focused on building a future with more security.

Yet a part of me still imagined being on stage like Jim Morrison from The Doors or being outrageous like Alice Cooper. If I had the musical talent my brother Jorge had, who knows where that road might have taken me? But now, Industrial Engineering was the plan. It was a path of structure and process, a complete contrast to the chaotic beauty of sound. I saw it as a way to apply creativity in a different form—one based on logic, efficiency, and improvement.

To feed my craving for the spotlight, I joined the theater class at school. We performed *Joseph and the Amazing Technicolor Dreamcoat*, and I played one of Joseph's brothers. Though the singing was pre-recorded and we only mimed and danced, I loved being on stage. The makeup, the lights, the energy of the performance—it gave me the adrenaline I had always craved.

One night after a show, I forgot my makeup remover cream. I tried to clean my face with water, but it only smeared the makeup further. With no choice, I walked through Saltillo with smudged makeup on my face. People stared. Some laughed. But I didn't care. I had been on stage, and the glow of that moment was worth every awkward glance.

During this period, I also asked my father to teach me how to drive. We had a Volkswagen Caribe with a manual transmission, and it was a challenge to master. But I learned, and the moment I was able to drive on my own, I felt a rush of independence. That sense of freedom—being able to go anywhere, do anything—was intoxicating. I only wished I had it earlier, especially the night I walked around town with that smeared stage makeup.

These experiences, both on and off stage, began shaping me. I realized that passion could come in many forms—not just through music, but also in solving problems, in storytelling, and in personal growth. I had started to define what would later become a driving force in my life: finding the balance between creative freedom and practical stability.

CHAPTER 7: INK AND IDENTITY

College was supposed to be a place for lectures, textbooks, and exams. For me, it also became a place for creativity, expression, and the unexpected thrill of influence. It started with a bulletin board in a quiet corner of campus and ended with me running the most talked-about student magazine in school.

The bulletin was basic—just a place to post class announcements, club meetings, and the occasional flyer about a missing textbook. I noticed it was often ignored, and I thought, Why not turn it into something people actually want to read? I had always enjoyed storytelling, designing things, and reaching people, and now I had a new playground. My idea was simple: take over the bulletin, give it a voice, and fill it with content that mixed popular culture with relevant student issues.

I taught myself to use early publishing software on the Macintosh computers in the campus lab—PageMaker was the tool of choice back then. I'd stay up late, tweaking layouts, creating graphics, and editing articles. At first, it was just me, but soon a few friends joined in. We started publishing short pieces—everything from "Top 5 Study Hacks" to interviews with professors who had cool hobbies outside of teaching. We even included short comics, jokes, and poems submitted anonymously.

Our little bulletin quickly turned into a mini-magazine. Students started looking forward to the new issues. I became the main writer, editor, promoter, and distributor. I'd print copies and leave them in high-traffic areas—cafeteria tables, student lounges, even taped inside bathroom stalls. I didn't care where people read it, as long as they did. And they did.

What made it work was the balance—we offered content that students actually cared about, but we wrapped it in creativity and humor. It wasn't dry. It was human. And that connection, that feeling of creating something that resonated with people, gave me a huge sense of purpose.

Unfortunately, like many passion projects, it relied on the passion of one. When I graduated, there wasn't anyone with the same drive to keep it alive. The publication faded shortly after I left. But its impact on me didn't. It taught me about initiative, branding, communication—and more than anything, about influence. I saw firsthand how ideas can spread, how something small can become something big, and how the right message, in the right format, can shape a whole community.

It also gave me a glimpse into what I would later do in the corporate world—building communications that connected people. The college magazine was the spark that lit a fire I would carry with me into every boardroom and factory floor.

Later in my life, I would create two additional magazines, this time geared towards promoting the company's achievements. I always believe in working hard but telling the world about it. Some of my publications were sent to corporate offices, other sister companies across different locations from USA to Germany, from Mexico to Brazil. Now is even easier to reach a larger audience through the different platforms; back then paper printing was the only option available.

CHAPTER 8: A FORGOTTEN APPLICATION

It was an ordinary afternoon in Saltillo when the phone rang and changed everything.

I had just come home from school, still carrying the usual weight of books and teenage concerns. My mother was in the kitchen, preparing dinner, and the smell of tomatoes and onions sizzling in the pan filled the house with warmth. The phone sat quietly on its stand, until it suddenly rang with a sharp jolt that echoed through the house.

My mother picked it up. I heard her voice change almost immediately—from casual to concerned, and then to something I couldn't quite place. Her eyes widened as she clutched the receiver closer to her ear.

"¿De verdad? ¿Estás segura, mamá?"

She listened in silence, nodding, and then her hand went to her chest. After a moment, she hung up and turned to me, her voice trembling: "Your grandmother just got the letter."

I stood there confused for a second, trying to process what she meant. "What letter?"

My mother didn't speak for a moment. Then she simply said, "Immigration. After ten years... we're next." I need to call your father.

I don't remember when the process first began, but my father submitted our family's petition in Piedras Negras when he was still working at Wrangler. Half of our family lived in Mexico, and the other half lived in the USA. I was just a boy then. Years had passed, and with them came doubt—maybe it was lost, maybe they forgot about us, maybe it would never come. But now, the waiting was over.

We had left Piedras Negras for Saltillo years ago, chasing work, stability, and a future. But my grandmother had stayed behind, keeping the house, the documents, and the memories intact. And now, in that house we had once called home, the letter had arrived. The envelope had our family name on it, written in formal print, like a summons from destiny.

My mother sat across from me, eyes glassy. "She said she didn't believe it either. She thought maybe it was a mistake. But it's real. We've been called. We need to get ready."

The air in the house changed. That letter felt like both a gift and a challenge. It meant the dream we had carried for so long—of moving to the United States, of starting again—was now within reach. But it also meant everything would change.

I thought of my grandmother in Piedras Negras, probably holding the letter in her calloused hands, reading every line slowly. I imagined her sitting at the kitchen table, the same table where we used to eat pan dulce and drink café con leche. I knew she must have cried, not just from joy, but from the memory of the years that had gone by without a word. She had kept our hopes alive, even when we stopped asking about the case.

The next day, my parents started gathering paperwork. My dad made a checklist. My mom called relatives. I remember her saying, "Your grandmother has kept every document perfectly. We just need to go get them." It hit me then—this journey had begun long ago, before I understood what it meant to leave a country, to start over.

That weekend we drove to Piedras Negras. The dusty roads, the familiar corner stores, the way the sunlight hit the trees in our old neighborhood—it all came flooding back. But when we got to my grandmother's house, everything felt different. She was standing on the porch waiting for us, holding that letter in her hand like it was made of gold.

She hugged each of us tightly, especially my mother. "I told you one day it would come," she whispered.

Inside, we sat at the kitchen table, and she laid the letter in front of us. I read the words carefully, the official stamp, the language I barely understood, and yet somehow I knew this was it. This was our bridge to a new life.

For my grandmother, it was more than a piece of paper. It was her legacy—proof that her faith and perseverance had paid off. For my parents, it was validation for the sacrifices they had made. For me, it was a beginning. One that would come with fear, excitement, and the bittersweet pain of leaving behind everything we knew.

That night, as we prepared to return to Saltillo, my grandmother hugged me and said, "Promise me you'll never forget where you came from." I nodded, tears in my eyes. "I won't."

The letter stayed behind for processing, but the dream it carried came with us. From that moment on, everything moved faster. Applications, interviews, passports, and planning.

We didn't know exactly when we'd leave—but we knew we would.

And that knowledge changed everything.

When we came back to Saltillo, we had a round table, My father asked, do we want to take this opportunity or continue with our lives here in Saltillo? This was going to be a democratic vote, my mom wanted to listen to us and then she would make her decision.

I was the oldest and I have the most memories of going to Eagle Pass, visiting my cousins in San Antonio, Texas, eating at McDonalds, and maybe the change to go and see Kiss in concert that would be so cool.

But, the most important thing, the United States was the land of opportunity, and if we worked hard, we could have a better future. I voted yes, let's go, my younger brothers followed up with a yes, and my mother wanted what was best for all of us. So, it was unanimous that we are going to United States of America, we will have our residence that took 10 years to come, but the possibility was here and now.

When the long-awaited letter from immigration finally arrived, it brought with it a mix of emotions—relief, anxiety, and anticipation. After nearly a decade of waiting, we had reached the next stage of the process. Our family—my parents, my younger brothers, and I—all went to the interview together in Ciudad Juárez. It was a moment we had envisioned for years.

At the time, I was 19 years old and just one semester away from graduating with my Industrial Engineering degree in Saltillo. I was excited, but also nervous. I knew this interview could change everything for us. We sat for hours in the waiting area, surrounded by others who, like us, carried the weight of dreams and sacrifice on their shoulders.

When it was finally our turn, the officer called us one by one. My parents went first. The officer asked them questions about their plans in the United States, who they knew, where they would live. My brothers were younger, and their path was straightforward. Then it was my turn.

The officer reviewed my file, flipping through the documents slowly. He looked at me over the rim of his glasses. "You're 19," he said. "Are you planning to finish school in Mexico or are you going to rely on the government here?"

I quickly responded, "I'm in my last semester of engineering school in Saltillo. I plan to stay and finish my degree. I am not planning to be living from the government, if we are planning to move to the united states is to contribute to be better for the country and for us."

He nodded thoughtfully. "That's good. I can grant your visa so you can visit, but for now, you will stay behind to finish your studies. Your parents and brothers will need to move to the U.S. immediately to activate their residency. Once you graduate, you can join them permanently."

It felt like a bittersweet moment. I was happy for my family, but also struck by the reality that I would be staying behind—alone. It wasn't common in Mexico for young adults to live on their own. I knew this would be a defining chapter in my life. My father looked at me with trust and resolve in his eyes. He said, "You're going to stay in the house. Keep the car so you can go to school. I have no money to give you. You're going to have to figure out a way to survive—sell things, find a job—do whatever it takes. But whatever you do, don't stop going to school. Get your degree."

I nodded. That was the plan. I helped them pack. We said our goodbyes. And just like that, they were gone. I stood in the doorway of our house, the silence settling around me, and asked myself: What now?

CHAPTER 9: CRAZY NIGHTS

After the structured life I had known growing up, moving to Saltillo felt like stepping into a new world—one filled with freedom, possibilities, and temptations. For the first time in my life, I was away from my parents and their rules. I had my own place, my own car, and the wide-open streets of Saltillo calling my name.

When Raúl moved in with me, things really took a turn. He had his own car, good looks, and an easy charm that made him popular with the ladies. We made a deal early on—if he was going to bring girls to party, he had to invite someone for me too. It was a handshake agreement that led to some of the most outrageous nights of my youth.

Our house quickly became *the* place for weekend gatherings. Loud rock music—Mötley Crüe, Twisted Sister, Ratt, Bon Jovi—pounded through the speakers. We didn't have much, but what we lacked in luxury we made up for in attitude. It was like living in one of those wild 80s movies—Porky's, Fast Times at Ridgemont High—except this was real. There were no parents, no curfews, and no limits.

I was only 19, and everything felt possible. We threw parties that lasted until the sun came up. The living room would turn into a dance floor, and more than once we ended up eating breakfast with strangers who had crashed on the couch. I didn't drink much—I never liked beer or drugs—but I was intoxicated by the thrill of it all: the music, the lights, the laughter, and the women.

Still, I never lost sight of my goal: to graduate. I knew I was walking a fine line between fun and failure. I was smart, and I could pick up on things quickly, so even if I skipped a class or two, I always did well on the exams. My grades weren't the best, but they were good enough to keep me moving forward. The freedom was exhilarating, but it was also dangerous. I saw people lose themselves in it. I didn't want to be one of them.

Raúl and I became legends in our own small circle. There was always someone stopping by our place, always a new adventure waiting. But with all that excitement came consequences. I hurt people I cared about. I made decisions I wasn't proud of. And yet, I wouldn't trade those memories for anything. They were part of my journey—part of learning who I was and who I wanted to be.

Looking back, that time in Saltillo was both a high point and a cautionary tale. It taught me the joy of living in the moment, but it also reminded me that freedom without purpose can be a trap. I survived that chapter with stories, lessons, and just enough sense to find my way back to the path I had always meant to walk.

In one of those crazy nights when I was driving down Victoria Street, the social heart of Saltillo where young people cruised back and forth in hopes of meeting someone new, a woman in another car shouted, "Hey, you forgot your sweater!" Confused, I asked what sweater. She laughed and admitted she thought I was someone else. Her name was Sandra.

She was older, confident, and strikingly beautiful. An architect with her own business and a sense of independence that stood in contrast to the girls my age. I was nineteen, unsure of what the next chapter of my life would bring, but there was something magnetic about her presence. She had her own office, her own life, and I was drawn to her. We began talking, and soon after, we were romantically involved. I didn't know at the time that this was going to be my first real relationship and that it would leave a permanent mark on me.

Sandra was ten years older than me, something that I initially brushed off, thinking maturity and independence were attractive. But as time passed, I began to realize that our lives were not in sync. While she was looking for stability and long-term plans, I was still discovering who I was and what I wanted.

I was living alone after my family moved to the U.S., and surviving on my own wasn't easy. I sold furniture to eat, party and afford gas, sometimes cooking hot dogs for dinner. Sandra, in many ways, was part of the stability I lacked—she often fed me, gave me a place to feel at home. But over time, the relationship began to shift. What once felt nurturing started to feel suffocating. Her desire for something more formal clashed with my increasing desire for freedom.

At the same time, I met someone new—Patty. Beautiful, kind, and smart. The moment I met her, something deep inside me said she was the one. I remember telling my friend Raúl that night, "She will be my wife." He laughed, but I knew it. The only problem? I was still with Sandra.

I tried several times to end things with Sandra, but every time I did, she cried, pleaded, and reminded me of everything we had been through. And I stayed. I didn't want to hurt her, and I didn't know how to say goodbye.

The breaking point came the day she discovered the letter Patty had written me. It was in my glove compartment, and when it fluttered out into her hands, I saw the storm come across her face. She read it, tore it to pieces, and threw it at me while I was driving. "You're cheating on me?" she cried. I said nothing. I couldn't argue. I just drove her home in silence. It was the last time we truly spoke.

Eventually, my family returned from the U.S. to help finalize the sale of our home. Sandra, being an architect, had promoted the house and found a buyer. She helped close the deal, and my parents gave her a commission. She asked why I hadn't come to say goodbye. They said

I was packing. But the truth was I couldn't face her again—not after everything.

Leaving Saltillo was one of the hardest and most necessary decisions I ever made. I didn't just leave a city—I left a life, a chapter, and the person I thought I'd be.

Looking back now, I see Sandra not as a mistake but as a deeply formative part of my story. She was a woman of strength, independence, and kindness. But sometimes love isn't enough when the timing is wrong, and you're walking different paths. My relationship with her taught me about emotional responsibility, the consequences of hesitation, and the courage required to move forward even when it hurts.

She wanted forever, and I wasn't ready. But I carry her memory with respect and the quiet knowledge that she helped shape the man I became.

CHAPTER 10: PATTY – THE HEART OF MY JOURNEY

Some people arrive in your life quietly, like a whisper in a crowded room. Others burst in like a firework. Patty was somewhere in between. The moment I met her, there was no thunder, no spotlight—just a gut feeling, a deep certainty that I had never experienced before. And I remember thinking: "She's going to be my wife."

It may have sounded like a joke to those around me—especially to Raúl, who laughed it off that night—but to me, it was a quiet truth I couldn't shake. Patty had a softness in her smile and a kindness in her eyes. She didn't need to be loud to command attention; she carried herself with a quiet strength and a dignity that made you want to lean in and learn more. I was 19, wild, untethered, living by myself, throwing parties with Raúl, and trying to figure out what the next chapter of my life would be. I had freedom, chaos, and temptation—but no anchor. Patty became that anchor.

She was older than me, a teacher, responsible, independent, grounded—and everything I wasn't at the time. But she never judged me. She saw through the noise and the distractions and chose to know me for who I really was, not who I was pretending to be at the moment. Our first months together were filled with long conversations, simple meals, laughter, and a growing sense of something real. I'd never met someone who made me want to become a better version of myself like she did.

Leaving Saltillo was one of the hardest things I ever did—not because I was afraid of the unknown, but because I was afraid of leaving Patty behind. That day I left, she cried. She didn't believe I would come back for her. But I made a promise. I would return.

We wrote letters. We called when we could. Time moved slowly. But we held on. I worked whatever jobs I could. I went back to school. I returned to Saltillo to see her as often as I could, sometimes scraping together the last of my savings just to spend a few days by her side.

I had always believed in gut feelings—the kind that hit you in the chest and don't let go. That was exactly what I felt with Patty. From the moment we met, I had a strong intuition that she would one day be my wife. I didn't know how or when, but the certainty was there—quiet, steady, and impossible to shake.

At the time, our relationship was still new. Life was complex, filled with the chaos of finishing my degree and figuring out what came next. But my heart was clear. One day, I sat down with Patty, looked her in the eyes, and made her a promise: "I don't know what the future holds, but I know this—you will be my wife." She smiled but didn't say much. I think she wanted to believe it, but she had her doubts. Still, I meant every word.

Not long after that, we made the bold decision to marry in secret. It wasn't the kind of wedding you see in movies—no grand ceremony, no reception—but it was full of meaning. My brother Alex stood by me as a witness, and I took Patty's hand with full conviction. We were still young, still learning, but we knew what we wanted: each other.

I was still finishing my Industrial Engineering degree in New Mexico, and the decision to marry without telling our families was not taken lightly. We were going against the grain, breaking unspoken rules in a culture that valued tradition and family involvement. But it felt right—for us.

Then everything changed. Sandra, who still lingered in the periphery of my life, found out about our secret marriage. Whether out of jealousy, spite, or a sense of betrayal, she went straight to my parents and told them everything. The news landed like a thunderclap. My parents were shocked, disappointed—not because they didn't love Patty, but because they felt left out of one of the most important decisions of my life.

The confrontation was difficult. I had always tried to live up to their expectations, to honor the values they instilled in me. But in that moment, I had to stand by my choice. I tried to explain that this wasn't an act of rebellion—it was an act of love and certainty. I loved Patty. I believed in our future.

Over time, the tension eased, and my parents came to accept the path I had chosen. But that period left a deep imprint on me. It was a moment of reckoning—between tradition and conviction, family and independence. And it reminded me that sometimes, following your heart means facing the consequences, standing your ground, and trusting that love will carry you through.

Looking back now, I still smile when I remember that promise. Because I kept it. Patty did become my wife—not just in secret, but in every way that mattered. And that promise, made from the heart, was the beginning of everything.

We married quietly at first, just by the civil registry. Later, we married again by the Church—on our own terms, with our own timeline. Patty planned every detail from Saltillo while I studied and worked in New Mexico. She never complained. She never asked for more than what we had. And she never let go of the belief that we were building something together, even when it was hard.

Patty moved to the United States with me. We didn't have much, but we had each other. We shared meals, paid bills, and figured things out one day at a time. She taught me how to slow down and appreciate the beauty of quiet moments. I taught her how to laugh in the chaos. Together, we created balance.

Through all the moves, job changes, sacrifices, and unknowns—Patty has been there. She followed me across borders, supported me during career shifts, stood by me when I doubted myself, and held our family together during every storm.

She is not just my wife. She is my foundation. My reminder that love is not about grand gestures or perfect timing—it's about choosing each other, every day, even when the path is hard.

If this book is the road of a dreamer, Patty is the steady, unwavering hand that kept the dreamer grounded. And for that, I am eternally grateful.

When Patty and I decided to have a proper Catholic wedding in Saltillo—one that honored tradition, family, and faith—it felt like a moment of convergence. We were no longer the young couple who had secretly tied the knot. We were now ready to celebrate our love in front of everyone who mattered to us. And when it came time to make the journey, I wasn't traveling alone—I was bringing someone unexpected: my Swedish friend Anna Lena.

Anna Lena and I had met at New Mexico State University. She was one of my new friends during a time of fresh starts, and we quickly bonded over our different perspectives and shared curiosity about the world. She was thoughtful, inquisitive, and carried herself with a calm confidence that made her easy to talk to.

When I mentioned I was heading back to Saltillo for my wedding, she lit up with interest. "I've never been to a Mexican Catholic wedding," she said with genuine excitement. "That sounds incredible." I hadn't planned to invite her at first—it seemed too far, too foreign—but she was thrilled by the idea and eager to experience something completely new. So I said, "Come with me."

We boarded a long-distance bus together from New Mexico to Saltillo. It was a trip filled with stories, laughter, and anticipation. She had questions about what to expect, and I tried to prepare her for the mix of tradition, ritual, and family warmth that would greet us.

When we arrived, Patty was already waiting. The moment she saw Anna Lena step off the bus with me, her face froze in surprise. I could read the question in her eyes before she spoke. "Who is she?" she asked, her tone cautious but curious.

I smiled and explained gently, "She's one of my new friends from school. She really wanted to see a Mexican Catholic wedding, and I thought—why not share this experience with her?"

Patty took it in, not quite sure what to make of it. But she trusted me. And soon, Anna Lena's grace and open-heartedness won everyone over.

She blended into the celebration with ease, absorbing every detail with admiration—from the elaborate religious rituals to the music, the food, and the joy that pulsed through every moment. My family welcomed her with curiosity, and she returned it with humility and appreciation.

Looking back, bringing Anna Lena to Saltillo was an unusual choice—but it was the right one. Her presence made the day even more memorable. It was a reminder that love, like friendship, doesn't have to follow a script. Sometimes it surprises us, crosses borders, and leaves a lasting impression.

In the middle of that traditional ceremony, surrounded by family and faith, there stood a guest from another world—honoring our culture, celebrating our love, and quietly making history in our story.

CHAPTER 11 : A NEW BEGINNING IN MESILLA, NM

Transitioning into professional life in the United States came with more than just a change in geography—it was a total shift in culture, communication, and opportunity. My first job in the U.S. was at a plumbing company, a far cry from the industrial engineering path I had studied for in Mexico. But it was work, and I took pride in doing it right. It didn't matter that I was driving a large truck or doing the heavy, dirty tasks most people avoided—I was learning, adapting, and slowly planting my roots.

From there, I took on extra jobs, even working at McDonald's to save money. My goal was clear: to return to Saltillo and see Patty. The distance had been difficult, and our relationship was built on letters and occasional phone calls.

Back in Mesilla, I was living with my parents again—something that tested my independence after years on my own. Our dynamics had shifted. I had matured, and they were learning to see me not just as a son, but as an adult. Despite our differences and occasional tensions, their support never wavered.

I returned to school with a renewed purpose. Classes were difficult, especially with the language barrier. I would translate my textbooks word for word using a dictionary—no Google Translate, no digital shortcuts. I took classes that relied heavily on numbers—math, physics, chemistry—because they were easier to follow and gave me time to improve my English.

Through it all, I made new friends from around the world—Spain, Sweden, South Africa—and they helped broaden my view of the world. These friendships, forged over late-night study sessions and shared frustrations, were an education in themselves.

One of the most impactful relationships I had during this time was with a young woman who had endured a great deal in her life. She was fragile and seeking connection, but also intelligent and kind. I helped her, and she helped me—particularly with my writing. She taught me to refine my English and express myself more clearly. Later, she would go on to write a book and build a life for herself in Germany.

As I juggled work, study, and marriage, I learned that success doesn't always follow a straight path. Sometimes, it looks like a plumber's wrench, a burger spatula, a letter from a loved one, or a hard-earned "A" on a physics exam.

I was building something—not just a career, but a future. And with every challenge, I felt a little closer to becoming the man I wanted to be.

I walked into the admissions office feeling a mixture of hope and vulnerability. My transcripts were reviewed, and I was told I would need to complete at least 30 credits to qualify for graduation from their engineering program. Each class counted for about 3 or 4 credits, so I needed to take around 10 classes, plus any additional requirements they saw fit. It was a long road ahead, but I was determined.

The advisor asked if I was comfortable taking classes in English or if I preferred ESL courses first. Always confident in my abilities, I told her I would go directly into the English-speaking curriculum. I selected math-heavy subjects at first—physics, chemistry, and calculus—because numbers, unlike language, are universal. But even then, it wasn't easy. I attended lectures, took notes I barely understood, and spent hours translating textbooks word by word with a Spanish-English dictionary.

During the day, I worked as a plumber's assistant. At night, I flipped burgers at McDonald's. And in between, I worked as a computer lab assistant at the university, helping other students with their projects. Every penny I earned went toward tuition, books, and the occasional long-distance phone call to Patty, who was still in Saltillo. I missed her, but our bond was strong, and we kept in touch with letters and the promise of a future together.

The university experience was unlike anything I had known. My classmates came from all over the world—Sweden, Spain, Panama, and South Africa. I learned about their cultures, their food, their perspectives, and this broadened my own view of the world. I was no longer just a Mexican student pursuing an engineering degree—I was part of a global tapestry, finding my voice in a new language, a new country, and a new future.

Slowly but surely, my English improved. I started participating more in class, making friends, and gaining confidence. What had once seemed like an insurmountable challenge was now a thrilling journey. Every late night of studying, every hour spent translating lectures, every small victory brought me closer to my dream.

Eventually, I completed the required credits and earned my U.S. degree in Industrial Engineering. Holding that diploma in my hand was more than just a personal achievement—it was a symbol of perseverance, sacrifice, and the belief that with enough determination, you can bridge any gap, overcome any language barrier, and turn any dream into a reality.

New Mexico State University wasn't just where I got another degree—it was where I learned how to survive and thrive in a new world. It was a place that tested me, challenged me, and ultimately helped me grow into the man I was meant to become.

CHAPTER 12: THE $1.5 MILLION LESSON

Fresh out of college with my newly minted Industrial Engineering degree from New Mexico State University, I was eager to begin my professional journey. I was hired by a large automotive supplier—Lear Corporation—as a cost engineer. The job was based in El Paso, Texas, but the facility I would be working with was across the border in Ciudad Juárez, Mexico. I was full of ambition and ready to prove myself.

The role involved estimating the cost of materials, labor, and overhead for automotive trim components—essentially all the coverings and cushioning for a car's seats. One of the first major projects I was assigned was a complete trim package for a three-row SUV for Chrysler. It included leather, cloth, and vinyl variations, and the quote I had to build would determine whether we won the contract.

Determined to impress, I dove deep into the bill of materials, organized each part into sections, and carefully reviewed every line item. I used a sheet of paper to go row by row, methodically checking off items to ensure nothing was missed. It was tedious work, but I was committed to doing it right.

I submitted the quote, and my supervisor and the engineering manager reviewed it. Everything looked good, and the bid was sent to Chrysler. It felt like a victory.

A few weeks later, Chrysler came back with changes to reduce the cost. It was time for a requote. I followed the same process as before, and this time noticed something odd—the leather version was more expensive than the original, despite the supposed cost savings. I compared the old and new versions and found the issue: in my first quote, I had missed a small but expensive leather component. It had been incorrectly categorized under retainers instead of leather, and my method of using a paper to check each section caused me to skip it entirely.

That tiny mistake—just $3 per unit—was multiplied across 500,000 units. The error amounted to a $1.5 million shortfall in our projected profits.

Panic set in. I knew I had to take responsibility. I drafted a resignation letter and took it, along with the corrected documents, to my supervisor. He was just as panicked as I was. "They're going to fire me," he said, staring at the documents.

"No," I replied. "This is my mistake. I'll take the blame."

He asked for time to think before we took it to our manager. The next day, I met with the engineering manager and laid everything out. I explained how the error occurred and handed him my resignation letter.

To my surprise, he pushed the letter aside. "You're not getting off that easy," he said. "You made a mistake, now you're going to fix it. You're flying to Detroit to explain to Chrysler what happened and come back with a solution."

That night, I booked my first solo business trip. No GPS, no smartphone—just a paper map, a sample trim part, and a determination to fix what I had broken. The next day, I walked into Chrysler's headquarters and presented my case.

They understood the mistake, but they wouldn't let us adjust the original quote. We had to live with it. That night on the flight back, I made a promise to myself: I would find a way to recover that $1.5 million. And I did. Over the years and through several re-quotes and adjustments, I gradually earned it back for the company.

The experience changed me. It taught me humility, accountability, and the true weight of responsibility. That mistake—my $1.5 million lesson—was the turning point in my career. It didn't end my journey. It started it.

After the incident that nearly cost the company $1.5 million, something unexpected happened — instead of being fired, I was given more responsibility. The leadership team saw that I had integrity, accountability, and the determination to own my mistakes and fix them. That earned their trust. Within a year, I was promoted to lead the cost department. The following year, I became the supervisor of both the cost and industrial engineering departments, and shortly after that, I was promoted again — this time to Engineering Manager.

I had climbed the ladder quickly, and while I was grateful, I started to notice something that didn't sit well with me. My salary had not kept pace with my growing responsibilities. Despite managing more people, bigger budgets, and having significant influence on the company's profitability, I wasn't being paid at the same level as the other managers.

I decided it was time to advocate for myself.

I scheduled a meeting with the director and came in prepared. I thanked him for the opportunities and growth, and then explained my concern. "I've looked at the salaries for engineering managers across the board," I said. "The entry point is around $50,000. I'm well below that, despite doing the work at that level for quite some time."

He nodded, acknowledging my point. "You've definitely had rapid growth here," he said. "And we've given you nice raises along the way."

I responded, "I appreciate those raises. But when you give 10% of a low number, it's still a low number. It doesn't bridge the gap."

He paused. "That's more than a 25% increase. It's going to be hard to justify."

I asked him, "If I left tomorrow and you hired someone new for my position, what would you offer them?"

He didn't have an answer, but we both knew the truth. They'd have to pay at least $50,000 — probably more — to bring in someone from the outside.

Still, he didn't offer to adjust my salary. I left the meeting disappointed but resolute.

I updated my resume and quietly started looking. I wasn't angry — just realistic. I wanted to grow, and I wanted to be compensated fairly for the work I was doing.

Soon enough, I landed an interview with another company — a foundry in Wichita, Kansas. They offered me the role of Industrial Engineering Manager and, without hesitation, $50,000 a year. That was exactly the number I had asked for.

With the offer in hand, I returned to the director. "I'm giving my two weeks' notice," I said.

He was surprised. "Why?"

"You remember our last conversation," I said. "I gave you the first chance to make this right. This other company doesn't know me, but they're willing to pay me fairly. I've given them my word."

He looked over the offer letter. "I'll match it — even beat it," he said. "$55,000 if you stay."

But I shook my head. "I appreciate that. But I already gave them my word. I'm not leaving because of the money anymore — I'm leaving because you only saw my value when someone else did first."

That was one of the hardest decisions I ever made, but it taught me a powerful lesson: Sometimes you have to bet on yourself, even when others won't. And when you do, you don't just get the salary — you get your dignity.

I made the move to Wichita, and that decision would shape the next chapter of my life.

CHAPTER 13: A MIRACLE IN WICHITA

When the opportunity to work in Wichita, Kansas arose, I saw it as a significant step forward in my career. I was taking on a challenging new role, leaving behind familiarity in exchange for growth. What I didn't know at the time was that Wichita would not only transform my professional life—it would also mark the beginning of one of the most cherished chapters of my personal journey.

Patty and I had longed for a child. When we first got married, doctors had told us that having children might not be possible. Patty had suffered a serious accident when she was younger—hit by a bus in Saltillo—and that trauma had shifted her internal organs in a way that made pregnancy unlikely. We carried this knowledge like a shadow, loving each other fully but with quiet acceptance that parenthood might never be part of our path.

In Wichita, we settled into a quiet rhythm. Patty took a job as a teacher's assistant while I immersed myself in the demands of managing an Industrial Engineering Department. Life was steady. Then, one day, Patty started feeling unusually tired and began gaining a bit of weight. I asked if she thought she might be pregnant, but she dismissed the idea. "You know that's not possible," she reminded me gently.

Still, I suggested we take a test. The result was negative. We moved on, but her symptoms continued. Another test. Another negative. Eventually, I insisted we go to the doctor. They ran blood work and, to our disbelief, the results came back positive—Patty was pregnant.

We were stunned. Elated. Disbelieving. It felt like a miracle we hadn't dared to hope for. Further examinations confirmed what we never thought we'd hear: Patty was four months along.

The news spread quickly at work, and my coworkers were just as thrilled. The team even threw us a baby shower. We were overwhelmed with gratitude.

When our daughter was born, I held her in my arms and felt a wave of emotions crash over me—relief, joy, fear, pride. She was perfect. We named her Anna Patricia. Anna in honor of my grandmother, who had passed away shortly after attending our church wedding in Saltillo. Her strength and faith had shaped me, and I wanted my daughter to carry a piece of that legacy. Patricia, of course, after her mother.

Anna's birth marked a turning point in our lives. Every sleepless night, every diaper change, every first smile and word reminded me of how far we had come—from dreams and sacrifices in Mexico to a new life in the United States. Wichita would forever be etched into our hearts, not just as a place of new beginnings, but as the city where our miracle was born.

CHAPTER 14: FORGING FLOW

My first challenge in Wichita was to improve the finishing department. Castings came from the mold line and moved into finishing, where operators had to remove flash, smooth out surfaces, and inspect for defects. The issue was that the process was broken into silos. Rough grinders blamed the belt grinders, who blamed inspection. Nobody owned the full part. Inventory piled up between stages. Quality issues multiplied. Every day, I walked into a game of finger-pointing.

I proposed something different: let's create a cell where a single operator—or a small team—would be responsible for all steps of finishing a part. Start to end. One continuous flow. No inventory build-up. No excuses.

Of course, there was resistance. The older operators didn't want to change. They were used to doing one task over and over again. Learn the belt grinder? "That's not my job." Work a different station? "I've done this for 20 years, I don't need to learn anything new." But the younger guys on third shift—they were different. They were hungry. Some were part of work-release programs, serving out the last of their sentences and trying to start over. They wanted the opportunity to learn, to prove themselves. So I started with them.

I trained them myself. I stayed late after shifts, running parts through the entire process. I showed them the results—how quality improved, how lead time dropped, how production went up. They bought in. And once they started outperforming the other shifts, the rest of the department took notice.

One day, during a meeting, a seasoned operator from first shift challenged me in front of everyone. "If you think it's so easy, why don't

you do it yourself?" I looked at him and said, "Give me two weeks."
I stayed after hours every day, practicing each stage—rough, belt, de-
tailed grind. I studied the standards. I timed myself. Two weeks later,
I ran the part in front of him and beat the standard. He looked at me,
shook his head, and said, "Okay... okay." And that was the day he became my strongest ally.

The success of the finishing cell became a model. The plant manager
called the owner, who flew in from Milwaukee to see it. After a tour
and conversation, he told me, "We've got another project. I want to
fly you to Oklahoma." That trip would change my life—and set the
stage for my return to Mexico.

But before that, I learned one important thing in Wichita's finishing
department: sometimes, you don't fix a system by patching it. You tear
it down and build a better one. And when you do it with respect, with
your own hands in the process, people follow you—not because they
have to, but because they believe in what you're building.

It was a crisp, clear morning when the plant owner approached
me with an unexpected proposal. He had just visited the newly implemented finishing cell and seemed visibly impressed. He had heard
about the improvements, the cultural transformation across shifts,
and the dedication we poured into that cell. With a firm handshake
and a curious smile, he said, "I'd like you to fly with me to Oklahoma."

I didn't know what to expect. I had never flown in a private plane before, and as we ascended above the Arkansas hills, the world below
seemed to shrink — yet the weight of possibility expanded in my
chest. The owner leaned toward me mid-flight and said, "I have plans
for you." Those words lingered in the air like the hum of the engine.

He explained that our company was entering into a joint venture with
a Mexican corporation to build a brand-new foundry in Monterrey.

The investment was massive — $70 million — and the mission was just as bold: to establish a world-class ductile iron foundry from the ground up. He wanted me to lead the industrial engineering efforts, to establish the systems and train a team that could bring this vision to life. It was the kind of challenge I had dreamed of.

As he laid out the plans, the wheels in my mind started turning. Saltillo. My wife's hometown was only 45 minutes from Monterrey. The place where our story began. Life had come full circle.

When I got home, I shared the opportunity with Patty. She had mixed feelings. On one hand, returning to Monterrey meant being close to family. On the other, we had built a peaceful life in Wichita. Family, while loving, can sometimes be overwhelming, and she was worried about how close proximity might impact our independence. Still, she supported the idea.

We relocated to Monterrey, I threw myself into planning. We began by assembling the right team. I took the new engineers back to Wichita to study operations firsthand and see what a successful system looked like. Back in Saltillo, we coordinated equipment installation, built bill of materials, wrote operational procedures, work instructions, and developed training materials. The dream was turning into a blueprint, and the blueprint was turning into reality.

We were preparing for our first ductile iron casting, a milestone that would prove whether everything we built could function under the pressures of real-world production. We marked the calendar: September 10, 2001. I was thirty one years old. My daughter had just been born. I was building a foundry — and a future.

Little did we know how drastically the world would change the very next day.

It was supposed to be a day of celebration. September 11, 2001, marked our first successful casting at the new foundry in Monterrey—a monumental milestone in a project that had taken months of planning, coordination, and relentless effort. The furnace had fired, the molds had held, and molten ductile iron flowed just as we had envisioned. That morning, I felt pride—not just in the work, but in the people who made it happen.

I woke up the next day ready to return to the plant and keep the momentum going. But nature had other plans. Heavy rain was falling, pounding the rooftops of Monterrey like a warning drumbeat. As I sipped my coffee and turned on the television, a local news broadcast showed footage of a school bus stuck near a flooded riverbed. Emergency crews were trying to help, and I remember thinking, Hopefully the rain stops soon—this is going to delay everything.

Then, the image on the screen changed.

The news anchor's voice faltered slightly as she reported a plane had hit one of the towers at the World Trade Center in New York City. At first, I thought it was an accident—some sort of tragic, isolated incident. I stood there watching, transfixed and confused. Then, live on television, the second plane hit.

That's when everything shifted. This wasn't an accident. It was an attack. The rain kept pouring outside, but it was nothing compared to the flood of questions and fear now spreading across the country—and the world.

The images that followed were burned into my memory. Smoke, fire, people running through the streets covered in ash. And then, the unimaginable: one of the towers collapsed. Minutes later, the second followed. I stood still, unable to move, my mind racing. Is this war? What happens now?

I thought of my family in the United States. My parents, my brothers. Though none of them lived near New York or Washington, I couldn't shake the fear that something could happen to them—or that our world had just become a much more dangerous place.

Despite the fear and confusion, I went to the foundry that day. But nobody was focused on castings or process flows. Everyone huddled around radios and televisions, trying to understand what had just happened. Phones weren't working properly. Borders were closing. Air travel was halted. It felt like the entire world had hit pause.

For the next several days, production came second to updates from the news. There was a strange silence in the plant, a heaviness that didn't lift for a long time. Though we were far from the epicenter of the attacks, we felt their shockwave just the same.

I realized something else during that time. For all the late nights and strategic plans, for all the talk of production volumes and efficiencies, there are moments in life when everything else falls away—and what truly matters comes into focus. That week, I thought about my daughter, just months old. I thought about Patty, and what kind of world she and I were bringing our child into. I thought about my team, many of whom were scared and uncertain, looking to leadership for answers none of us had.

The ramp-up continued, of course. Business always does. But something had changed—not just in the world, but in me. I understood with greater clarity the weight of responsibility I carried, not just for operations, but for people. Real people with families, fears, and futures. The kind of understanding that no MBA program or engineering manual can teach.

The world never returned to what it was before September 11, and neither did I. But from that day forward, I carried something deeper in my leadership: a sense of urgency not just for performance, but for presence. To be there. To connect. To protect. Because when everything else falls away, that's what really matters. I truly believe in the saying that "united we stand, divided we fall".

CHAPTER 15: BACK TO WICHITA

After spending several transformative years in Mexico managing the foundry start-up, the time had come for another chapter. We returned to Wichita, Kansas, and although I was seen as the turnaround expert, I was no longer thrilled by the work. My reputation had earned me the responsibility of resolving ongoing third-shift issues, but something felt off. In Mexico, I had been the Foundry Manager, fully in control and making a direct impact. Now, back in the U.S., I was simply a night-shift troubleshooter, once again disconnected from my family due to the odd hours. I found myself sleeping when they were awake and awake when they were asleep.

Then, life changed in an instant.

My mother called with the news that shattered my world—she had been diagnosed with cancer. Her voice on the phone carried worry, but she was strong, even in that vulnerable moment. I knew right away what I had to do. No job, no title, no responsibility could compare to the need to be close to my parents. I started looking for opportunities closer to them and eventually found one: a Maintenance and Engineering Manager position at a company manufacturing vacuum cleaners with aluminum die-cast operations.

It wasn't in the same city, but it was close enough. We made the move, and just like that, I turned in my two-week notice.

At first, the new role was a change of pace. It lacked the adrenaline and challenges of turnarounds or start-ups, but it offered something I hadn't had in years: time with my family. My daughter and I developed a close bond—we played video games together, shared music, and watched movies. She had a friend named Crista, and I loved hearing them laugh in the other room. Life was calm. My mother's treatment brought her cancer into remission, and for a while, it seemed we had all taken a collective breath.

But deep inside, I was unfulfilled.

The job didn't inspire me. It was predictable, repetitive, and lacked the sense of urgency and purpose I thrived on. I found myself slipping into a quiet dissatisfaction. The excitement that once fueled my career was missing. Even with the joy of being with my family, something was off balance. I wasn't learning. I wasn't growing. And as time passed, that emptiness started affecting my mood.

One day, I had a realization—I could not continue living a life that dulled my passion. I had done what I needed to do for my family, especially for my mom. But now that her health had stabilized, it was time to find something that would reignite my spirit.

I began to look again—not just for a job, but for a mission. I wanted to transform another plant, help another team, and make an impact. I wanted to be the person who could once again take chaos and mold it into clarity.

Because that was who I was.

And deep down, I knew there were still roads ahead waiting to be traveled.

Still, I stayed in this role for six years. I did good work, launched new models, and made meaningful improvements. I supported my mother through her treatment, which, miraculously, brought her cancer into remission. And once the family was in a better emotional space, Héctor began to feel the old itch return—the hunger to build, fix, and lead.

The spark hadn't died. It had simply rested, waiting for the next fire to ignite.

CHAPTER 16: FIRES, FORGING, AND BROTHERHOOD

The Springdale forging facility in Arkansas was unlike any place I had ever worked. With its enormous layout, it buzzed with constant energy—26 forging hammers pounding metal into shape, heat treatment furnaces glowing with intensity, and plating lines humming with activity. You could walk through the plant and feel the heartbeat of American manufacturing, raw and unfiltered. This place had a certain grit to it, the kind that came from decades of tough work and tighter deadlines.

I came in as the Maintenance Manager with one mission: to establish a culture of predictive and proactive maintenance. But that was easier said than done. The plant was always so busy that maintenance often became an afterthought. Equipment was repaired only when it broke down, preventive tasks were skipped, and oil-soaked residues in critical areas were left unchecked.

The most alarming issue was in the heat treatment area. The process required heating metal parts and then dipping them in oil to change their molecular structure for durability. Over time, oil vapors collected on the ceilings and walls, turning into a ticking time bomb. It was only a matter of time before something went wrong—and it did.

One day, flames erupted from the heat treatment area. I saw fire rising 50 feet high, licking the ceiling with terrifying force. The evacuation alarms sounded, and chaos rippled through the plant. But I couldn't just walk away. My team, my friends, the very livelihood of hundreds depended on that facility. I told my team to grab the extinguishers and ropes. My maintenance supervisor Brian and I climbed to the roof.

We formed a human chain, pulling up fire extinguishers one by one as I tried to control the flames until the fire department arrived.

The plant manager, also fairly new, climbed up and helped. Amidst the smoke and heat, he turned to me and said, "How did we end up here?" I looked him in the eye and replied, "We're here because we care. And I promise you, this will be the first and last time we'll ever be up here."

After the fire was out and the dust settled, we launched a full investigation. The long-time employees weren't surprised—they said a fire happened about every two years. That shocked me. It wasn't just a maintenance issue; it was a cultural one. I dug deeper and discovered the root cause: the exhaust stacks had wood frames under the stainless steel exterior. Years of exposure to extreme heat had dried the wood, turning it into flammable charcoal.

I proposed a solution: remove all wood around the stacks and rebuild the structures entirely in stainless steel. We also scheduled deep cleans of the ceiling and walls every six months, non-negotiable. It wasn't cheap, but the leadership team approved the plan. From that moment forward, the facility never saw another fire of that kind.

But that wasn't the only fire we'd face. Another incident occurred in the forging area. A hydraulic hose burst on one of the forging hammers, spraying oil that caught fire upon contact with a 2,200°F billet. The sprinklers activated, soaking the shop floor. As we scrambled to control the fire, I asked Brian for a "wet-vac." My accent twisted the words, and in the middle of the tension, he jokingly replied, "Why do we need more wetbacks? We already have you."

It was a joke, perhaps a risky one, but in that moment, we laughed. The tension broke, and we got back to work. That was Brian. Big, smart, committed, and someone who knew how to lighten the mood when it mattered most. He became my right hand in transforming the plant's safety culture and maintenance discipline.

But change was in the air. A new plant manager arrived—one they called the "Angel of Death." A corporate leader tasked with quietly transitioning production overseas. I didn't know what was coming, but I could feel it in my gut. The days of this old powerhouse were numbered.

CHAPTER 17: THE ANGEL OF DEATH.

As I continued to lead improvements in the Springdale forging facility, a new figure arrived from corporate—someone everyone referred to as "The Angel of Death." I had heard the nickname whispered with unease in the hallways, but I didn't fully understand it until the day I was summoned to his office.

He was calm, almost too calm, as he laid out the plan. My task, he said, was no longer to build a sustainable maintenance program or ensure long-term equipment health. Instead, my mission was now to prepare the entire facility for closure. Every machine needed to be brought to top condition, not for longevity, but to be disassembled, crated, and shipped overseas. Most of the forging lines would be relocated to Taiwan, while a smaller portion was bound for Mexico. The goal was clear: within three to five years, this plant would no longer exist.

The news hit me like a sledgehammer. I had just spent months of my life pouring energy, time, and leadership into transforming the culture of this facility. I had built strong relationships, developed trust, and mentored individuals who had grown into leaders themselves. And now I was being asked to help dismantle it all.

When I returned home that evening, I sat down with Patty and shared everything. She could see the frustration and sadness in my face. "I know what this means to you," she said. "But you've always done the right thing, and whatever you decide—I support you."

At work, I couldn't tell my team the full truth. The long-term vision I had been preaching no longer applied. Preventive and predictive maintenance felt hollow, knowing that within a few years, the machines would be gone and so would the jobs. But I continued to lead as best I could because the people still deserved my respect and commitment.

I began to see the writing on the wall. Though I was offered the chance to stay on and assist with the overseas transition, everything in my gut told me this wasn't my path. It wasn't that I was against change or international work, but this didn't feel like growth.

I couldn't be part of a process that would ultimately devastate a community I had come to care deeply about. I updated my résumé and began quietly searching for new opportunities—ones that aligned with my values and allowed me to build, not dismantle.

Sometimes, leadership means knowing when to walk away from something, even if it's running well, because it no longer fits who you are. This was one of those moments. I had to move forward, but I knew I would carry the faces, the stories, and the spirit of Springdale with me wherever I went next.

CHAPTER 18: THE ROAD TO REDEMPTION

Leaving the forging facility behind, I stepped into a new chapter—one that took me to the state of Nevada. I accepted a position at an aluminum casting facility in Carson City. The work was challenging in its own way, but less intense than the fire-prone chaos I had left behind in Arkansas. For a brief time, I thought I might have found a new professional home, a quieter stage to apply my skills. But fate had other plans.

While I was settling into this new role, I was persistently contacted by a headhunter. He had found my profile and was convinced I was the perfect fit for an opportunity with a global German-based company. This company operated two major manufacturing sites—one in Michigan and the other in Mexico. I told him I had just started this new job and didn't want to appear disloyal or like a job-hopper. The timing wasn't right. But he kept calling.

Finally, I brought the situation up to my wife. Her advice was simple and wise: "Just go and see. You never know—it might be something great." So, with cautious optimism and a little guilt, I agreed to visit the company.

During the interview process, I met with both plant managers. The position was for a North America Director of Maintenance. My role would be to improve performance and reliability at both locations. I'd be based in Michigan but would spend significant time in Mexico. I asked where in Mexico, and the answer stunned me—Saltillo. The very place where my journey with Patty had started.

I requested to see the Saltillo facility before making any decisions. A trip was scheduled for a weekend so it wouldn't interfere with my current job. But the trip was a disaster logistically. My return flight from Saltillo was canceled due to dense fog, so I drove to Monterrey and caught a flight there. I arrived in Las Vegas late at night, only to discover the rental car I had reserved was unavailable. The company upgraded me to a white Ford Mustang, a small silver lining.

I drove through the night, navigating lonely desert roads and passing Area 51. I didn't stop until I reached home. After a quick shower, I went to work as if nothing had happened. I told myself that no matter what, responsibilities must come first.

The Saltillo facility impressed me. It was clean, well-organized, and filled with potential. Patty and I discussed the opportunity. Our daughter Anna was having a tough time in school in Nevada, and this new adventure might help her reconnect with her roots. We decided to take the leap.

We moved to Port Huron, Michigan—right on the border with Canada. It felt poetic. I was born and raised on the border between Mexico and the U.S., and now I was beginning a new chapter at the U.S.-Canada border. A full-circle moment that felt like it was written in the stars.

CHAPTER 19: A NEW LIFE AT THE NORTHERN BORDER

Settling into Port Huron, Michigan, felt like a symbolic new beginning. It was a town on the edge of the United States, just across the bridge from Sarnia, Ontario, Canada—cold, quiet, and unfamiliar. From the warm familiarity of the Mexico-U.S. border, we had now landed on the doorstep of a different world, yet the parallels were not lost on me. Just as my childhood had been shaped in the shadow of one international border, here we were again—starting anew, thousands of miles away from home, but still straddling two cultures, two countries, two identities.

Our new home was modest but comfortable, and more importantly, it represented stability. For my daughter, this was a chance to further develop her English, to settle into a new school system, and to rediscover her own bicultural identity. Patty, ever the pillar of support, helped ease the transition. Though she had concerns about being far from family again, she embraced the adventure with me. She had done it before, and we had survived. Now, it was our daughter's turn to learn and adapt.

After a smooth first year working as the North America Director of Maintenance, things took a dramatic turn. A major quality issue erupted with one of our largest automotive customers. It wasn't just a minor inconvenience—this was a full-blown crisis that risked millions in contracts and the reputation of both the U.S. and Mexican facilities. Leadership needed someone to take control, find the root cause, and regain customer trust. That someone was me.

I took ownership of the issue immediately. I gathered both plant teams—Mexico and the U.S.—and began a deep dive into the process.

It became evident that the root cause stemmed from a misalignment between quality standards at both facilities. While the equipment and systems were top-notch, the alignment between people, training, and execution was inconsistent.

I initiated daily cross-functional meetings, aligning quality, maintenance, and production teams to rapidly address the problem. We implemented a containment process, temporarily modifying production so every part was triple-checked. At the same time, we launched a complete retraining program to standardize procedures. I met with the customer's quality team myself, explaining the steps we were taking and building their confidence day by day.

The pressure was immense. This was more than just solving a technical issue—it was about restoring faith. Within weeks, we turned the corner. The defective rates dropped, customer satisfaction began to rebound, and margins started to improve.

Soon after, the CEO from Germany reached out. He had seen the numbers, heard about the recovery, and understood the leadership it took to drive such results. He asked me to take over as the interim Plant Manager in Saltillo to help stabilize and restructure the entire operation.

My wife and I had an important conversation. Anna was still in school in Michigan, but Patty and I both felt this could be a unique opportunity. She believed Anna could benefit from being immersed again in her Mexican roots, and that returning to Saltillo—even temporarily—could be good for all of us.

And so, we packed up our lives and returned to Saltillo. But this time, the story was different. I wasn't a young man chasing a dream. I was a seasoned leader, bringing two decades of cross-border industrial experience back to the city where everything began for Patty and me.

At the Saltillo plant, I focused on restoring team morale and rebuilding operational discipline. I set clear expectations, reestablished accountability, and reintroduced performance metrics across all departments. I split my time between Saltillo and occasional visits to the U.S. facility, supporting both operations while reinforcing a unified culture.

What made this transition even more meaningful was Anna's reaction. She was now a teenager, fluent in both English and Spanish, and though she had grown up mostly in the U.S., she quickly adapted to life in Mexico. She reconnected with her roots and developed a deeper appreciation for where her parents came from.

I had come full circle. I was once the boy from Piedras Negras who watched the U.S. from across the border with curiosity. Now I was a leader moving between countries, bridging cultures, building teams, and carrying the responsibility of hundreds of employees.

Though the road ahead was still filled with challenges, I felt deeply aligned with my purpose. Not every story has a perfect arc, but this chapter reminded me that sometimes you need to return to your roots to truly understand how far you've come—and how much you still have to give.

Working for a German corporation meant frequent trips to Europe—factory visits, executive meetings, and long days spent between airports and conference rooms. The pace was intense, but every once in a while, I found time to breathe. On one of those business trips, I made a decision: I would take a couple of days for myself and visit Prague.

I had heard about its beauty, of course—but nothing prepared me for what I found. Prague, to this day, remains the most beautiful city I have ever visited. There was something magical in the air—the quiet poetry of cobblestone streets, the elegance of Baroque facades, the mystery of winding alleys that seemed to whisper stories from centuries past. The architecture, the mood, the balance of grandeur and stillness—it was all perfect.

As I walked through Old Town, I eventually found myself standing before the Astronomical Clock Tower. I took a seat on a nearby bench, letting the moment settle around me. Tourists gathered for the hourly show, cameras ready. The mechanical figures began their dance—death ringing the bell, apostles appearing one by one, the golden rooster crowing. It was beautiful. Mesmerizing. Ancient.

But my mind wasn't on the clock.

I sat there, watching it all unfold, and suddenly a thought hit me with full force: *A kid from dusty Piedras Negras made it here.*

Every decision I had made—every risk, every heartbreak, every victory and failure—had led me to this exact place, in this exact moment, watching this ancient clock mark time in the heart of Europe.

I wasn't supposed to be here—not by the odds, not by the statistics. But here I was.

I thought of my father, working long hours at the Wrangler jeans factory. Of my mother, raising three boys with quiet strength. Of the boy I once was—curious, restless, dreaming of a world beyond the border. And now, here I sat, halfway across the world, wearing a business suit and reflecting on a life that had taken so many turns.

It was a moment of deep gratitude and quiet awe.

Not for money. Not for success. But for *the journey.*

In that instant, I realized how far belief and persistence could take someone. From the warm, dusty streets of Piedras Negras to the cold stone beneath my feet in Prague—this was the path I had carved. Brick by brick. Decision by decision.

It was never just about work, or travel, or even the clock itself. It was about stopping time just long enough to reflect, to honor the road behind me—and to remind myself that I was still moving forward.

I had dreamed of taking Patty and Anna to Europe for years. After spending so much time traveling on business—often alone—I wanted them to experience the places that had inspired me, the stories hidden in the streets, and the beauty that can't be captured in photos. So we made it happen. We packed lightly but carried the weight of excitement, curiosity, and long-held dreams.

We flew into Frankfurt, Germany, where our European adventure began. At the airport, we rented a car and set off—not knowing we were about to drive over 4,000 miles across the heart of Europe.

Our first destination was Prague, a city that has always held a special place in my heart. From there, we continued to Vienna, where the elegance of the past seemed to linger in the air. Then came Venice, where we floated through canals and got lost in alleyways filled with music and art. Florence welcomed us with Renaissance beauty, and Rome overwhelmed us with history. The Vatican left us speechless in its sacred grandeur, and Pompeii brought us face-to-face with ancient tragedy frozen in time.

After Italy, we crossed into the south of France—visiting Cannes, then winding our way through Grenoble and Lyon. Each city was a new chapter, a new flavor, a new rhythm. But it was Paris that called us to stay.

Paris became more than just another destination—it became our reward. Our rest. Our reflection.

Mornings were spent with fresh croissants, afternoons wandering through museums or watching boats on the Seine, and evenings soaking in the lights of the Eiffel Tower. Patty found joy in the charm of every street corner, and Anna's wide eyes took it all in like it was a dream come true.

I wanted to keep going—to push farther, to see more. But my girls were tired. They didn't want to rush anymore. They wanted to live in the moment, not just pass through it. And so, I listened.

Sometimes, the greatest gift you can give your family isn't more places—it's more presence.

We spent our final days in Paris simply being together. Laughing. Walking. Eating. Remembering. And when it was time, we got back in the car and drove the long road back to Frankfurt—4,000 miles behind us, and a lifetime of memories within us.

That journey taught me that the real landmarks are not the ones you take pictures of—they're the moments when you pause, look at the people beside you, and realize you've arrived somewhere beautiful together.

CHAPTER 20: A DREAM FULFILLED

A few months after returning from our Europe trip, life seemed to settle into a comfortable rhythm. But then came a phone call that would once again shift the course of our family's story. My mother called—my father had suffered a seizure while eating. He had never had one before and, for a few minutes, didn't recognize her. Alarmed, they sought medical help. A battery of tests followed. The diagnosis was devastating: three tumors in his brain. Aggressive cancer. Inoperable. The doctors estimated he had three months left—six if radiation helped.

My father was 74. Before this, he had been active, sharp, and full of life. I rushed to their home to be with them. He was still conscious, still the father I remembered, though now burdened with the knowledge of what lay ahead. He had decided not to pursue radiation. He wanted quality over quantity. But my mother pleaded with him to try—to stay with her just a little longer. He eventually relented and agreed to the treatment, not for himself, but for her.

I returned to work, haunted by the image of my father grappling with his mortality. I remembered a dream he had always carried: to one day drive a red Stingray Corvette. He never did—life's responsibilities always took precedence. But I could do something. On my next trip to visit him, I rented the closest thing I could find—a red convertible Camaro. It wasn't a Corvette, but it would do.

When I arrived, he didn't recognize me at first. But his eyes lit up at the sight of the car. "Wanna go for a ride?" I asked. My mom protested—he couldn't drive—but I reassured her that he would just ride shotgun. We hit the road, my father in the passenger seat, my nephews and niece in the back, and we cruised through downtown Amarillo. For those few hours, he was a different man—smiling, laughing, wind in his hair. That ride was one of the last good memories I shared with him.

I told my brother Jorge to call me when the time came. A few months later, he did. The doctors had said it wouldn't be long. All of us gathered at his bedside. We said our goodbyes. When he passed, my mother cried out, begging him not to leave her. He stirred for a moment, as if her voice had brought him back. I gently told her, "You have to let him go. He needs to rest. Don't worry—we will take care of you."

He passed peacefully. At his funeral, some of his former coworkers came and shared stories of Mr. Ibarra—the leader, the mentor, the friend. I was proud of the legacy he left behind. He had not only provided for his family but had impacted so many lives. My journey had always been driven by a desire to honor him, and in that moment, I felt both grief and gratitude.

After my father's passing, the house felt quieter. The air was heavier with silence and the absence of his voice echoed through every corner. My mother, though strong, was clearly heartbroken. They had shared a life of more than four decades together. She had lost her life partner, her confidant, and her daily companion. I knew I needed to do something to help her navigate this new phase of her life.

I told my brother Jorge that I was going to take our mother back home with us for a while. My hope was that distance from the memories etched in every wall of their house might help her breathe a little easier. Before we left, I asked Jorge to change some things in the house—rearrange the furniture, repaint the walls, anything that would help soften the memories when she returned. The idea wasn't to erase the past but to give it a new lens, one less painful to look through.

At our home, we did our best to keep her occupied. We took her out, showed her new places, and did everything we could to bring a little joy back into her days. One night, as we watched a classic film together, she spoke about her love for music and movies. Her eyes lit up, and she shared something I had never heard before—her dream had always been to go to Paris. My father had promised to take her one day, but life, responsibilities, and finances got in the way. That promise was never fulfilled.

My father's dream may not have come true exactly as he imagined it, but in a way, it did. And in honoring his dreams, I found more clarity for my own.

Some promises are made with words. Others are made with love—and kept in silence until the right moment comes.

Months later, after his passing, I decided it was time. My mother had given everything to our family, and now it was my turn to give something back. I told her we were going to Europe—not just for the sights, but to walk the path my father never got to walk beside her.

We packed our bags and flew across the Atlantic. It was more than just a trip—it was a tribute.

Our journey took us to places she had only imagined: the old cathedrals of Germany, the charming streets of Italy, the sweeping history of Nuremberg. But it was Paris that brought the dream to life.

Paris was where my father's spirit felt closest.

As we stood in front of the Eiffel Tower, my mother's eyes welled up with tears. She didn't say much. She didn't have to. I knew what it meant to her. And I felt something too—not just pride, but peace. Because in that moment, I knew we had completed something. We were not just tourists. We were carrying out a wish left behind.

That trip reminded me that love doesn't end with goodbye. It continues in the promises we keep, in the dreams we carry forward, and in the memories we create on behalf of those who couldn't.

For my mother, it was a journey of healing. For me, it was a way to say thank you—not just to her, but to my father, for everything he had done and all that he still inspires me to do.

We walked, we laughed, we cried. And when we came home, we brought more than souvenirs. We brought closure. We brought light. And we brought the quiet satisfaction of a promise fulfilled.

After the trip to Europe with my mother, something in her changed. She came back to her home calmer, lighter in spirit, and filled with gratitude. The adventure we shared had honored my father's memory in the best possible way—not with mourning, but with movement, discovery, and a fulfillment of the promise he once made to her. The promise to take her to Paris was no longer unfulfilled. In a way, he had taken her there—through me, through our shared love and commitment as a family.

When she returned home, she was greeted not by the same heavy echoes of loss, but by a space that felt slightly different. My brother Jorge had followed my suggestion—he had rearranged the furniture, painted the walls in fresh colors, and made subtle changes to help ease the emotional burden of returning to the house where she had spent decades with my dad. It was still their home, but now it had a new rhythm, a new tone. She was not starting over, but continuing on, with new memories to carry her forward.

Looking back, that journey with my mother was more than a vacation—it was a closing of a chapter, a bridge between past and future. It was about healing, honoring, and finding joy again. She had always been the quiet strength behind our family, and now it was my turn to be that for her. I took care of her as she once took care of me, and in doing so, I felt closer than ever to both of my parents.

Life moves forward, but some promises echo across time. And when you fulfill them—not just in word, but in action—they become eternal.

Returning from our second Europe trip, life seemed to settle into a steady rhythm. My mother, now more at peace after seeing the places she once dreamed of, went back to her home. Anna, however, began to struggle with cultural differences after our move back to Mexico. She faced harsh bullying from classmates, mostly centered around her Spanish. Though she understood and spoke the language, her sentence structure was reversed—thinking in English while writing in Spanish, which is not an uncommon challenge for bilingual children.

Despite her best efforts, some peers were relentless. The teasing, the nicknames, and the constant need to prove herself took a toll on her confidence and joy. One day, she came to me and said, "Dad, I want to go back to America. This isn't for me. I want to finish high school in the U.S. and start college there." I knew she had thought it through. I asked her if she'd decided on a career path. With conviction in her voice, she said, "I want to be a veterinarian."

Patty had a friend who worked as a vet, and I asked if he could allow Anna to shadow him at the clinic. He agreed but made it clear that it would be unpaid. That was fine by me. I just wanted her to get a real taste of the field. Anna dove in. She helped clean cages, assist with minor tasks, and even observed surgeries. One day, I asked her, "So? Is this what you want to do?" She smiled and said yes—then added, "But there's something I won't do."

"What's that?" I asked.

"I'm not going to declaw cats or cut dogs' tails or ears. It's cruel. It's not about the animal's health—it's about aesthetics or convenience for the owner. I can't support that."

I admired her principles, but I was also realistic. "You know that could hurt your business," I said. "If you don't give customers what they want, they might go elsewhere."

"I'd rather do something else," she replied firmly. "Maybe zoology. I can work with animals in nature, study them, protect them. I'll still be helping them, just in a different way."

It was clear she had not only passion but also clarity. I told her, "If that's what you want, go for it."

Anna's journey reminded me of my own: a path that twisted and turned, led by conviction and values. Watching her find her own way filled me with pride. She wasn't just learning from life—she was shaping her own story, just like I had shaped mine.

I talked to Management and we relocated back to Port Huron for Anna to attend the last year of high school and get ready to go to college and pursue her passion as a Zoologist.

At work, things were going smoothly, and then another challenge would come our way.

Leadership is tested not in calm seas but in storms. During the COVID-19 pandemic, we faced a storm like no other.

When the new German CFO joined the company, he brought with him a sharp financial mindset, a polished resume, and an outsider's view of how things should run. On paper, he was exactly the kind of leader our multinational operation needed—data-driven, pragmatic, and disciplined. But what he lacked was understanding. Not of numbers, but of people.

As the virus spread and borders began to close, our leadership team faced critical decisions. Travel plans were canceled. Budgets were frozen. Employees worried about their health, their families, and whether they'd even have jobs tomorrow. It was chaos. And in that chaos, a single decision revealed everything about our new CFO's leadership style.

We had a maintenance engineer—a hard-working, humble man from our Mexico plant, the company offer him a work visa, he moved with dreams and hopes, when he moved his wife was pregnant and now, she had a newborn—he had move to our Port Huron facility to support a major equipment installation. He was skilled, reliable, and deeply committed. But then the world shut down, and he was let go. I reached out to my own pocket and help him and his family to return to Mexico, we went to the Mexican consulate, we got a passport for his new born baby and he and his wife flew back to Mexico. The engineer and I, we rented a Uhaul and we drove from Michigan all the way to the border so he could bring all of his belongings back home.

He was not the only one; by this time all the operators had been laid off, and the engineers, managers, including myself, were doing double or trip duty.

The CFO next step was, we need to cost more costs, he asked me you need to cut everybody salary by 30%, I did not agree, I told him, this people are already making jobs that were not in their job descriptions, the expectations was to do their jobs and also be operators and they were doing it, the morale was still good, but if I told them this we will lose all loyalty to the corporation, I told him, nothing last forever and once this pass by, we will need their support to rebuild.

He did not agree, I had worked hard to build a team, but plant managers were properly trained, since I express my opinion, the next day I was let go, no thank you for 6 years of work, no thank you for all the new business, sales and profits that I brough, no bonus that I had earned before Covid hit, no vacations, no severance package. Nothing.

That moment taught me something important: a title doesn't make you a leader. Your decisions do. Your empathy does. Your willingness to see people as more than lines on a spreadsheet does.

In times of crisis, real leaders show up. They don't hide behind policy. They roll up their sleeves and ask, 'What do our people need right now?'

That experience stayed with me—not just because of what happened to him, other people, and myself, but because it reminded me why I lead the way I do. People first. Always.

CHAPTER 21 – THE ROAD AHEAD

As I sit here reflecting on the road I've traveled, it's hard not to feel a deep sense of gratitude—for the struggles, the triumphs, the unexpected turns, and the quiet moments of clarity. From the dusty streets of Piedras Negras to boardrooms in Germany and beyond, my journey has been one driven by dreams, defined by decisions, and shaped by resilience.

Now, as Chief Operating Officer of a company that values people as much as performance, I finally feel like I've reached a place where both heart and mind are aligned. I am part of a team that believes in connection, culture, and vision—not just numbers and charts. It's a rare alignment in the corporate world, and I cherish it.

But my journey isn't over.

I may be 55, but in many ways, I feel as energized as I did at 25—still learning, still dreaming. With 10 to 15 years left in my professional career, I want to spend them not just achieving, but mentoring. Helping others rise. Building legacies that outlast any title.

At home, my daughter has grown into a thoughtful, driven young woman. My wife continues to be my anchor, my partner, my reminder of where we started and why we've endured. And I carry with me the memory of my father—his sacrifices, his strength, his promises. His journey lit the path for mine.

Life has taught me that the road doesn't have to be perfect. It just has to be yours. And as long as you keep walking it—with integrity, purpose, and an open heart—you're already successful.

This is not the end of my story. It's simply the closing of one chapter...

and the anticipation of the next.

The road of a dreamer never truly ends. It just continues—carved by vision, lit by hope, and traveled with courage.

ACKNOWLEDGMENTS

First and foremost, I want to thank my wife, Patty, for her unwavering love, loyalty, and strength. You have walked beside me through every chapter of life—through struggles, victories, uncertainty, and growth. You are the heart of my story, the calm in my chaos, and the steady hand that held mine when the road was hardest. To my daughter Anna, thank you for inspiring me every day with your curiosity, intelligence, and compassionate heart. Watching you grow has been one of the greatest joys of my life.

To my parents, whose sacrifices laid the foundation for everything I have achieved. Dad, your quiet work ethic and commitment taught me what it means to be a man. Mom, your resilience and boundless love were a guiding light through every storm. I carry both of you with me in every step I take.

To my brothers Alex and Jorge, thank you for the laughs, the support, and the memories we share. You are part of every stage of this journey, and I'm proud of where we've all come from—and where we're going.

To the mentors, teachers, coworkers, and friends who shaped my character and career: your lessons—both direct and indirect—helped forge the person I became. Thank you for the opportunities, the challenges, and the belief you placed in me.

And finally, to everyone who took the time to read this book: thank you for joining me on this journey. I hope you find in these pages not just my story, but reflections of your own.

This book was made possible by memory, perseverance, love—and a dream that refused to quit.

ABOUT THE AUTHOR

Héctor Ibarra is an International Impact Book Award–winning author and a respected operations and manufacturing executive. His leadership career spans multiple countries, guiding teams through plant launches, organizational transformations, and large-scale operational turnarounds.

Born in Mexico and now leading in the U.S. manufacturing sector, he brings a cross-cultural perspective shaped by resilience, humility, and a lifelong commitment to growth.

His debut memoir, *The Road of a Dreamer*, lays the foundation for his next book, *Dreamers Who Lead*, a leadership memoir exploring the principles behind high-performance teams and authentic leadership in today's world.

Learn more at: www.theroadofadreamer.com

PHOTO INSERT: MOMENTS ALONG THE ROAD

My mother and father: the heart and backbone of everything I am.

The longest days were the happiest. We played in the dirt without worries, not knowing we were planting the values that would sustain us for life.

Patty and I on the streets of Saltillo, where our story began with silent promises.

A simple, deep, and eternal love. A 'yes' that united us forever.

Anna Lena, my Swedish friend, visiting Saltillo. She joined us for a Catholic Mexican wedding and shared memories that blended two cultures.

A look that lights up the room. My reason to keep dreaming.

A dream is not built alone. This team marked a turning point in my professional life.

My adventure through Nevada, right before I started the next chapter at work.

A dream fulfilled. My mother at the Eiffel Tower—the promise my father couldn't complete, we made real together.

www.ingramcontent.com/pod-product-compliance
Lightning Source LLC
Chambersburg PA
CBHW070635130626
46555CB00006B/2561